PRAISE FOR

It's Never Too Late To Dance

"Rosann is one of the most joyful people I've ever met."
—Ann Curry, NBC Anchor, *Today* and *Dateline NBC*

"I've known Rosann Levy for fifteen years, and I can tell you first-hand that she is the perfect person to take us all for a ride on life's dance floor. Her story will inspire everyone who reads it."
—Bobby Flay, Chef & Restaurateur

"Rosann Levy has written a poignant memoir of a life lived for the love of life. This is a courageous woman who sometimes resembles Indiana Jones in her strength, poise, and remarkable gift for overcoming seemingly insurmountable adversity. *It's Never Too Late to Dance* is an inspiration for anyone who had even the remotest thoughts about giving up and of not believing that no matter the cards you are dealt, you too can write a lot of stories with happy endings."
—Danny Meyer, CEO Union Square Hospitality Group and author of *Setting the Table: The Transforming Power of Hospitality in Business*

PRAISE FOR

It's Never Too Late To Dance

"If anyone knows how to live a life full of bombastic creative energy, it's Rosann Levy, mother, businesswoman, entrepreneur, and grandmother all rolled into one self-satisfied and dynamic package. Rosann seamlessly floats between projects making each step seem as if it is both loaded with dynamite and never-ending pleasure."

—Patti Greaney, Executive Producer of Giraldi Media, Founder of StarChefs.com and Founder of Out of Hand Festival

"Rosann Levy is a wonderful storyteller with a warm, accessible voice and an imaginative style. This is a triumphant tale of over-coming personal demons and living life to the fullest. Readers will relate to her big dreams and even bigger heart as she traverses the challenges of building a family, two family businesses, and ultimately her own truth."

—Cris Beam, author of *Transparent*, Lambda award winner and Stonewall Honor Book

"A humanistic journey of her life, Rosann's memoir is motivational and an inspiration to people of all ages."

—Neal Goldberg, President and CEO, Zale Corporation

PRAISE FOR

It's Never Too Late To Dance

"Reading this book as both business woman and friend, I applaud her openness, her ability, and her sensitivity in dealing with the many problems faced by business families. The readers will nod their head 'yes' as they relate, but also they will gain perspective and hopefully new solutions as they attempt to build and sustain their own businesses."

—Helene Fortunoff

"An evocative story that tells of real life experiences and confirms the highs and lows that face us all during our lifetime... A must read."

—Wolfgang Brendel, World Renowned Opera Star

"I have met very few people in life that have Rosann Levy's passion for living. She is a modern day Renaissance woman who loves and nurtures her family and friends; intelligent and business savvy and open minded to a whole array of possibilities. She is a rare gem in this world and her story inspires us all."

—Mitchel Bleier, Internationally Recognized Yoga Master,
MB Yoga

7/13/10

Rick,

It's
Never
Too Late
To
Dance

On!
Keep
Dancin'!
Rosemary Leny

ALSO BY

—◆—

Rosann Levy

Family Business Magazine
"Growing the Firm—and Growing the Marriage"

Building Strong Family Teams
"Rosann Levy Wins Equality in Her Husband's Firm"

It's Never Too Late To Dance

A Memoir

By

Rosann Levy

Legwork Team Publishing
New York

Legwork Team Publishing
80 Davids Drive, Suite One
Hauppauge, NY 11788
www.legworkteam.com
Phone: 631-944-6511

First edition 7/9/2009

ISBN: 978-0-9841-5350-3 (sc)
ISBN: 978-0-9841-5351-0 (hc)

Printed in the United States of America

This book is printed on acid-free paper.

Illustrations by Christopher Donovan

For Arty:
my husband, my soul mate and
my best friend

Contents

Acknowledgments

There are many extraordinary people in my life who have helped me grow to who I am today. Without their advice I'm not sure I would have been able to accomplish building three successful businesses. I am grateful to have had mentors, business colleagues, friends, and family members as a part of my life. They have helped me raise four children, overcome insecurities, and become a successful business woman.

It's Never Too Late To Dance has been a labor of love for the past three years, and it is at this time I want to thank the people who supported me in this effort.

Cris Beam, my writing teacher and my coach, challenged me, questioned me, and pushed me to improve my writing, assuring me of writing a better book. Without her guidance and patience I would not have been able to complete this task. She believed in me and taught me the artful skill of writing, and to her I am forever indebted.

I want to thank Lori Gershon who introduced me to Yvonne Kamerling and Janet Yudewitz of Legwork Team Publishing who made my book a reality. Their support, advice, and knowledge are unrivaled and I am thankful they kept me on a deadline. I am also grateful to the entire Legwork Team; the editors who read the manuscript with a fine-tooth comb and the illustrators who made the illustrations of the dancers jump off the pages.

Thank you also to my dear friend, Joan Lieberman, who spent her entire Christmas vacation pouring over my manuscript.

A particular thanks to my sister, Irma Zigas, who reminded me about some of my early years and brought them to life. She has always been there for me and I am humbly grateful.

It is with my deepest gratitude that I thank my husband, Arty, who continues the journey with me after more than fifty years. It is a wonderful journey. He read, reread, and critiqued every chapter, making sure I recalled and was accurate about our lifetime experiences. Without his inspiration, support, and love, I never could have written this book. Arty has taught me how to take risks and supported all my endeavors to become an independent woman. I admire, respect, cherish, and love him and his devotion to our children and grandchildren.

I must give a special thank you to my children and their spouses, Mitchell and Jill, Gary and Robyn, Kenneth and Barbara, and Tracy and Mitchel, for their undying love and support and for putting up with some of my crazy antics.

I especially thank my children for giving Arty and I our most precious gift: our nine grandchildren. Kaely, 17, has grown into a beautiful young woman; her sister, Nikki, 14, is a caring, sensitive, and sweet teenager who excels in anything she sets her mind to; Charlie, 12, is an articulate young man who I believe will be President one day; his brother Lucas, 9, is a talented musician and great athlete; Andrew, 8, with the most amazing imagination has the smarts to become a top-notch doctor; his brother Michael, 5, whose upbeat energy lights up a room and his athletic ability is already quite apparent, Alexis, 6, with her beautiful red hair has the poise and grace of a famous actress; her sister Amanda, 3, who shows signs of being a great leader in whatever endeavor she chooses; and our newest edition, Beck with his big blue eyes and his sweet smiles that bring even more joy into our lives. Watching our grandchildren grow and discover the world is our greatest pleasure.

Introduction

"My Life's Journey To Empowerment and Change"

*I*n my life there is much that I've accomplished. I've become a successful owner of three different businesses in New York City, worth million of dollars. I've been the President of the National Association for Women Business Owners, the Founder and President of the Family Business Council of Greater New York, and I have made countless appearances on TV and radio. In direct contrast to these achievements, I've had numerous emotional setbacks and difficulties. I've been afraid to walk down my own stairs for fear of getting a knife from my kitchen and stabbing myself in the gut. I also faced my own mortality after lapsing into anaphylactic shock— a trigger for months of agoraphobia and deep depression stemming from early childhood traumas. Even more heart wrenching was when my son was diagnosed with cancer. There is nothing more shocking and painful than to deal with your child's mortality. However, these life-threatening experiences taught me how to value my life, adapt to change, appreciate my family, and know the true meaning of life itself.

It's Never Too Late To Dance tells the story of my journey. It's a memoir about business successes, depression, learning to cope with cancer in the family, and how I ultimately built a more meaningful life. This story bares my soul, offers up my passions and joie de vivre, and will educate the thousands of women who are unhappy, struggling with their inner truths, and seeking happiness, but aren't sure how to find it.

I am a woman with no formal educational training. My only experience with college was attending New York University for one year. I am also a woman who built a premier New York City accounting firm, Arthur D. Levy & Co., into a multi-million dollar business that served thousands of clients. After twelve years, I sold the business to one of the top twenty-five accounting firms in the country. The sale of both this business and the Family Business Council secured retirement for me and my husband and enabled us to open a Latin Ballroom dance studio in the heart of New York City, where people can smile and enjoy one of the many pleasures of life. Now that we are in our "golden years," we are delighted that we can share our passion and love of dance with people of all ages, shapes, and skills.

Ballroom Dancing

"While we may not all be leaping around into our nineties, dancing is one activity we can (hopefully) do for the rest of our lives... and the social aspects are all part of its allure. It's a great way to make new friends, be creative and expressive, and just plain old enjoy life. And, the best part of dancing is the fun you can have while you're doing something great for your body because your heart and bones don't know whether you are jogging, in the gym or dancing!"

—David Robinson, EZinearticles.com

— · ♪ ♪ ♪ · —

Fox Trot

The Fox Trot is considered to be
the most significant development in ballroom dancing.
The dance's combination of quick and slow steps
encourages flexibility. As a romantic dance,
the Fox Trot is a preferred first dance
for couples on their wedding day.

Escape

**A progressive, traveling dance,
the slow-slow—quick-quick steps of the Fox Trot
would be influential in guiding us along our own
dance floor as we began our dance of life together.**

He pressed his soft lips against mine and kissed me. It was our first date. After our high school basketball game ended, eight of us piled into a friend's 1950 light green Ford Coupe. I squeezed into the backseat and sat on Arty's lap. The pressure of his hand resting between my shoulder blades pulled me close, and without warning he kissed me gently. I had never thought of Arty as a romantic partner, yet instinctively I closed my eyes. He continued with more fervor and I responded. Arty was different than the other boys I had dated. His kiss was gentle, yet protective. It was as if my heart told me he would take care of me forever. He would be my escape from my abusive father.

- ♪ ♪ ♪ -

Rosann Levy
_____

I was born September 24, 1941 in Freeport, New York, the third child of Ruth and James Greenhut. My mother, who gave birth to me at age thirty-nine, wanted a namesake for her mother, Rose, who had recently died. Having already raised two children, my mother pulled away from the daily routine of childrearing and focused on her social life. She relied on my sister, Irma, and brother, Martin, who were twelve and seven years older, to be my caretakers. But my siblings were busy with their friends and didn't want their kid sister tagging along. The combination of my siblings' rejection and my mother's active social life made me feel unwanted through much of my early childhood.

My father wasn't attentive either. He was too busy working. His loud gruff voice was intimidating, and he ruled the house like a dictator. He was short man with broad shoulders and a mustache that resembled Hitler's. He frightened me. It was as if every time he opened his mouth I was expected to raise my right arm and salute him. I remember him reprimanding me when I was afraid of a thunder and lightening storm. "Get into bed," he'd shout. Hearing him yell as I stood at the top of the stairs, I became hysterical. Suddenly he ran up the stairs, swatted me on my backside, pushed me to my room, and slammed my door. I cried myself to sleep. I often escaped to a neighbor's yard, where I'd sit under a big willow tree. I'd tug lightly on a branch as if I were holding my friend's hand and look at the billowing clouds protecting the heavens. I silently prayed, wishing I had a different father.

My father was born in Budapest and immigrated to the United States in 1907, when he was four. I imagine he felt threatened by the great hall at Ellis Island with its twenty-foot ceilings, heavy wood paneled walls, and the long line of people waiting for officials to stamp the required documents. I have heard the story often, and I can envision my father stepping up to the desk, holding a worn canvas satchel in one hand and his father's hand in the other. When the immigration officer asked his name, my father had responded in his broken English,

"Imre."

The officer shouted impatiently, "What?" My father repeated "Imre" again and again. The officer stamped the paper work with a heavy hand, looked at my father, and said, "OK, OK, your name is James."

And from that day forward my father's name was James.

Being the oldest of four siblings in a poor family, my father was forced to leave high school and look for a job when he was only fifteen. He resented this and became a lonely, self-taught man, who escaped later in his life by reading National Geographic and watching public television.

As a kid, I never knew when my father would become enraged and lash out. Chore time was a common fuel to his ire; as I vacuumed the living room rug, he'd pick up the side chairs, shove the end tables out of my way, and yell, "any dummy can do it." I'd cower yet act quickly so as not to disappoint him.

Sometimes my mother protected me. Once, when I was scouring a frying pan, my father chased me to the basement with a dish towel, yelling that it wasn't clean enough. My mother followed quickly, stepped between my father and me, and put her hands up to shield me from his wrath. I remember tugging at her apron strings until he walked away.

My father's behavior was different with my mother. Longing for her love and attention, he'd respond favorably to her every whim. "Jimmie," she'd call in her high pitched voice, when she wanted him to complete a task, and he'd jump up and change the light bulb, fix the leaky pipe, or plunge the stuffed up toilet. Unfortunately my mother was blind to his need for love and put us kids first, which made my father jealous, so much so that he acted harshly and verbally abused his children.

When my mother ignored my father, he would retreat to his workshop in the basement of our home to expertly repair old furniture with his "golden hands." I remember watching him carefully glue the legs of four matching oak antique chairs. As he tightened the clamps, the thick transparent substance dripped onto the newspaper he draped on the floor. Once the glue dried, my father turned them upright and sat on each of them, making sure his work was sturdy. The furniture was the outlet for his desperation to be heard by my mother.

Unfortunately retreating to the basement was not the only way my father would satisfy himself; taking to the bottle was another. His drinking brought on crying jags and always scared me. During these bouts with tears, my mother would go to his side. They never argued—the battles were between my father and us kids. My brother, a weak individual, always followed my father's orders. My sister, on the other hand, was defiant. When I was eight, I watched my father verbally attack my sister because he didn't approve of her boyfriend—he had been drinking. The argument got out of hand, and he chased my sister upstairs with a broom. Overwhelmed with fear, I ran to a friend's house hoping my parents couldn't find me.

Perhaps my mother was able to be softer with her children because she came from a close-knit family with hardworking parents. She was of Russian descent and immigrated to New York with her family as a very young child. Like my father, she was the oldest of four siblings but she wasn't forced to be their caretaker. Her father owned a candy store on Tremont Avenue in the Bronx called Comras Candies and Treats, which provided him with the means to feed his family. I remember visiting there as a child; my grandpa would sit on an old wooden milk crate at the front door. He had big blue eyes, thinning grey hair, and a welcoming smile. Even though the store was small and dark, the energy inside was upbeat with racks of comic books: *Wonder Woman, Felix The Cat, Little Orphan Annie,* and more lined the walls. I reached for the comic with Popeye carrying Olive Oyl in one arm while downing a can of spinach with the other. Flicking through the pages, I laughed at the cartoons of Popeye making googly eyes at Olive Oyl playing with Sweet Pea. With her nose shaped like a pickle and a heart that was fickle, she was Popeye's "goil"—her only competition was his spinach.

Comras Candies was a hangout for neighborhood kids. The candy treats, baseball cards, yo-yos, water guns, toy soldiers, and other playthings my grandpa had placed in small bins in front of the cash register were a big attraction. I loved going there—it was like being in Willie Wonka's Chocolate Factory. Just like Charlie was with his grandpa, I was with mine. The sweet scent of chocolate candy filtered through my nose, and my mouth watered as I quickly reached for the Milky Way and 3 Musketeers Bars, my favorites.

Rosann Levy

My mom was a short stocky woman and walked with a limp—family legend says she was hit by a trolley car crossing the street in the Bronx not long after she immigrated to New York—yet it never took away from her beauty or her flirtatious personality. She had a creative flair and liked trying new things; oil painting classes were a favorite. She was not into high style fashion, yet when she spent the summers at her bungalow in Long Beach, she wore the newest trends in swimwear—the stretch tummy control which held in her stomach and emphasized her bust-line.

She colored her short curly hair with Clairol products. I remember her using a small red handled brush stuck in a six ounce juice glass in the bathroom, the stiff bristles awry from its constant use. I was fascinated, watching her pouring the black dye into the glass and then painting her head. Her colored hair always made her look younger; I imagine she thought this made her more attractive, especially to men, as she enjoyed many male friendships. I don't want to believe there were any romantic encounters, but I can't be sure.

Even though I felt my mom wasn't as available for me as I would have liked, I migrated toward her—I felt safe with her. I would emulate her flirtatious encounters and used similar tactics to attract boys as I entered my teen years. I learned I could be in control by being sexy. Because my father dubbed me the "dummy" early in my childhood, I believed I wasn't smart. To overcome my poor sense of self, I used my sexuality to entice boys to like me.

- ♪ ♪ ♪ -

In eighth grade, I was chosen to be president of the "boy's club." There were eight of us, and I was the only female in the group. We discussed everything from sports to cool local hangouts. I felt accepted and my dependency on my relationships with the group grew as my sexual attractiveness increased. I wore poodle skirts with tucked in, tight fitting blouses, accentuating my curvaceous body hoping to attract even more attention. As my popularity increased, my confidence rose. Soon I had more dates than I could handle, which sparked me to buy a dress and shoes for the senior prom before I was even asked to attend the event.

In ninth grade, I joined a group of girls known as the "Sexy Individuals" (SIs). The SIs were very popular and we loved dating senior boys who were known as the "Freshman Lovers." It was then that I met Arty; he was one of them. Whether at basketball games, high school socials, the movies, or Lucy's, the local ice cream parlor, we were inseparable. Flirting was our favorite pastime.

Teenagers in the 1950s represented a generation of innocence, before the sexual revolution took hold in the 1960s. Music from rhythm and blues to jazz to the introduction of rock and roll influenced the teen culture. Movies like *Teacher's Pet, Singing In The Rain, The Pajama Game* and television shows like *I Love Lucy* also played a part. The media affected our social interactions, and kissing, hugging, and other forms of physical affection were done blatantly in public—school hallways, cars, movie theaters, and other local hangouts. Necking and petting led to further sexual relations and gave guys bragging rights using baseball terms to confirm their sexual accomplishments—1st base, 2nd base, 3rd base, and a home run. In spite of this, virginity was still considered a virtue, and girls who went further than 2nd base were known as "sluts."

The relationship between me and Arty reflected the dating customs of the time. I remember one night Arty parked his car on a dark dead end street, a hangout for lovers. Occasionally there would be other cars parked in the darkness, but this night we were alone. We began necking which led to heavy petting—our body heat fogged up the windows. All of a sudden, we heard a knock on the driver's side. My heart palpitated. Arty quickly zipped up his fly as he opened the window. It was a policeman shining a flashlight in our eyes.

"What are you doing here? Do your parents know where you are?" the cop asked. "This is a private road. You kids better leave before you get into more trouble."

My hands were shaking. Arty nodded his head at the officer, apologized and told him we were on our way home.

- ♪ ♪ ♪ -

Whenever I saw Arty, I noticed that his smile lit up his face as he hung out with friends in the halls of Malverne High School, in Malverne, New York. At six foot three, he had a tall lanky build, a chestnut brown crew cut, brown eyes, seductive sexy lips, and he smelled like Old Spice. I didn't think Arty was my type since I was normally attracted to dark haired, rugged, macho guys. In contrast, Arty's soft features radiated good character, intelligence, and confidence. His persistence in getting to know me aroused my curiosity. I watched from my front door as he drove up to my house in his brand-new 1955 red and white Dodge. Relaxed with his shoulder leaning against the door and his left hand resting on his chin, he exuded a confidence that excited me. He honked the horn, and I quickly ran to him as if he were a superhero waiting to take me away on an adventure.

Our dates were typical of those in the 1950s—drive-in movies where we'd hook up with friends and mix the alcohol stash with grape juice and other sweet combinations; basketball and football games where we'd fill coolers full of beer and cheer on our home team. I remember going to parties where romance was the theme—we'd dance to the make-out music of Nat King Cole and Frank Sinatra and bump and grind slowly to a sexy dance called the Fish.

After dating for a few months, Arty asked me to go steady and gave me his senior class ring. Accepting this confirmed our commitment, letting everyone know that we were dating each other exclusively. I wore the ring proudly on a long chain around my neck for everyone to see. Our intimacy gave me security, increased my self esteem, and made me less dependent on my parents. I was ready to explore the significance of our connection.

As our relationship grew, my mother developed a fondness for Arty. She observed that he was respectful, protective, and truthful. Their weekly card games reinforced her favorable opinion; my mom loved to play and Arty was a card fanatic—gin rummy was his favorite game and he enjoyed taking her on. They played for nickels, but watching them play you'd think they were playing for millions.

Arty's mother died when he was seventeen, and I believe that the relationship with my mother helped fill that void. His mother had been sick with Hodgkin's Disease for seven years. His father, Jack, was a selfish man. He was angry that he was saddled with a sick wife for so many years and had to care for children he didn't want. He was unable to administer the daily morphine shots to relieve his wife's pain and burdened his son with this horrific task. Having no other choice, Arty became a caretaker when he was only ten years old. Perhaps this caused him to take on the caretaker role with me. Having grown up in an authoritative environment. I welcomed his caretaking. He made me feel secure and loved. I, in turn, supported his every need and provided him with unconditional love, something he had not received from his parents.

Arty was emotionally scarred from caring for his mom and then watching her slowly die, but his pain deepened when his father married a woman named Sylvia only four months after the death of Arty's mother. Arty resented the marriage and wouldn't accept Jack's new wife. Sylvia had her own son, and five years later, she and Jack had a son together. She showed no interest in caring for Arty or his younger sister, Joan. Arty thought of Sylvia as the wicked stepmother. She treated him with disrespect and convinced Jack to make Arty sleep in the basement. She gave her son the biggest room on the second floor. Since Jack had suffered by having a sick wife for so long, he granted Sylvia her every wish. She continued to find ways to demean Arty by humiliating him in front of his friends for not completing chores, saying he was "a lazy bum." I remember watching her run after him with a rake, chasing him from the yard because he didn't walk the dog. She was nasty to me and snubbed me when I came to visit. She made it clear that I was not good enough for Arty because I came from what she categorized as "a poor family." She convinced Jack to feel the same way she did and forced him to write Arty a letter stating if he were to marry me, I would ruin his life.

Arty's mild temperament turned into rage as he read the harshly worded letter, his father handed him when he was home from college for the Christmas break. He later told me that he confronted his father and had to restrain himself from punching him in his jaw and reiterated his screaming match.

"How could you write something like this? You don't even know Rosann! You're the one who is ruining my life!"

Storming out of the house, Arty immediately came to see me. Frustration overwhelmed him as he smacked his fist down hard on the desk in my bedroom. He grimaced with pain as he covered his face with his hands to hide his tears. I hugged him.

"I can't stay there. I won't let him or his disgusting wife control me or control us. I will find a way to get out of that house. He's not even paying my college tuition....why do I need him?" He shook his head in disgust.

But Arty didn't have to wait for very long. When he returned home, his father stood in the doorway with Sylvia shadowing him. His arms were folded across his chest as if he were a drill sergeant.

"You're not welcome here!" Jack said. "Pack your bag and get out. GET OUT NOW!"

"You're throwing me out?" Arty asked. "I guess I should thank you. For the first time in my life, you are doing something good for me."

Arty pushed his father and Sylvia into the wall to get them out of his way and ran to his room in the basement. He quickly threw some clothes in a bag and had a friend drive him to the home of his maternal grandmother, where he lived until we married. Still yearning for her father's love, Arty's sister, Joan stayed in the house with Jack and Sylvia.

- ♪ ♪ ♪ -

Growing up in such a tumultuous home environment, Arty had no choice but to be a risk taker. He sought ways to defy authority and was decisive and creative in planning mischievous pranks. His friends followed his lead. They stole a bowling ball from the local bowling alley, just to annoy the owner, and moved a street stop sign from one location to another to confuse drivers. These tricks secretly excited me. Perhaps his pranks thrilled me because I grew up in a house controlled by a dictator and I would have been beaten if I rebelled. Secretly I loved the excitement, and his crazy ways also showed me a more macho side, someone who I thought was more my type. I fell in love with a prankster, who was caring, loving, and very supportive.

Once Arty moved into his grandmother's house, he took on a few part-time jobs during holiday and summer breaks from college in order to create some financial stability for himself. During his first Christmas recess from college, he took a job as a shoe salesman at Baker's Shoes in the Green Acres Mall in Valley Stream, NY. After one week of training, he asked me to stop by the store to test his shoe-fitting skills. I smiled as he put black suede pumps on my feet. Pressing his thumb at the tip of each shoe to make sure my big toes had enough room, he asked me to walk slowly across the room and tell him how they felt. For an instant, I pictured myself as Cinderella trying on the glass slippers. They were a perfect fit and I was his first paying customer.

The following summer, he took a job pumping gas on Sundays at a Mobil gas station, which was close to the mall. The big rectangular sign boldly showcasing the flying red horse above the storefront brought back a fond memory of my father's bedtime stories—Princess Pee Wee and her flying red horse. As a child, these were rare, gentle, and happier moments I spent with my father and the only times I looked forward to being with him. I enjoyed his magical tales. He'd describe how the flying red horse would sweep the Princess to fantasy lands where she would reign as queen; she'd fly in amidst a crowd of little people resembling the munchkins from munchkin land in the *Wizard of Oz,* waving and cheering her arrival, and she showered them with toys and candies. I'd visualize being the Princess—it made me feel loved. Arty's knock on my window brought me back to reality. "How much?" he asked me with a smile. "Fill her up," I said.

It was 1958. "True Love," a hit song from the popular movie, High Society, was our theme song. Arty loved to sing and he sang romantic songs periodically that expressed his feelings. Driving to our favorite parking spot to neck, Arty smiled as he hummed the music from "True Love." He parked and turned off the headlights. Cupping my face in his palms, he kissed me softly. "I love you," he said as he took a deep breath. Suddenly, he took out a small black velvet box tied with a white ribbon from his jacket pocket. He looked at me with adoring eyes and presented me with this tiny package.

My hands were shaking as I started to untie the bow. Lifting the lid I saw the one-carat diamond in a Tiffany setting sparkle.

Arty took the ring from the box and placed it on the ring finger of my left hand. "Will you marry me?" His voice quivered. Without hesitation, I put my arms around his neck and shouted with glee, "YES, YES, YES!"

We kissed and held each other close for what seemed like hours. He later told me it had been his mother's engagement ring.

- ♪ ♪ ♪ -

The relationship between Arty and my mother grew. I remember my mother looking at Arty with a big smile on her face, tapping him on his shoulder, and telling him, "I trust you, I know you will take good care of Rosann." Yet my father and Arty had no connection whatsoever. It was only after I had a fight with Arty that I had an opportunity to have a serious conversation with my father. Arty and I disagreed about our wedding. I wanted a big wedding, but he was adamant about keeping it small, no more than fifty people. The argument escalated and ended with me slamming the car door and running into my house crying hysterically. My father stood there at the front door and in an uncharacteristically compassionate voice said, "Let's talk."

With tears streaming down my face, I looked at him quizzically. He took me by the hand and we sat down on the front stoop. The night was clear with stars lighting up the sky.

"Are you sure Arty is the one? Do you believe in your heart he will make you happy?" As if he were reciting wedding vows, he continued, "Will he love you in sickness and health, will he care for you no matter what? Do you love him?"

I sat silently and let his words fill my head. His compassionate voice made me feel calm, a feeling I was not used to. Holding my hand in his, he told me that he only wanted me to be happy. I saw him as a different person that night. Instead of instilling fear in me, he comforted me.

"Arty is a good person," I said. "He puts me on a pedestal and makes me feel special. He treats me with respect and is responsive to my every need. I feel safe with him, and I know in my heart he will take care of me," I told him. "He truly loves me as I do him. I hope you get to know him like I do."

I reached out and hugged my father. The man I thought of as an ogre had finally showed me he cared.

Arty and I got married on December 26, 1959. Immediately after the ceremony my father reached for Arty, shook his hand, and said, "Welcome to the family son." I smiled as I watched the two embrace. Looking behind me, I saw Arty's father and Sylvia cowering in the corner.

I don't recall if Arty and I danced the Foxtrot that night, but I knew that our dance of romance throughout our lives together was just beginning.

- ♪ ♪ ♪ -

Lindy Hop

The Lindy Hop became a dance craze, worldwide,
known as the Jitterbug. It evolved into
the West Coast Swing, and at parties
people would often break out into the lively dance.

Sex, Drugs, Rock 'N Roll & Babies

**Dancing to the beat of our own drums the
Lindy Hop got hotter and hotter as we embarked
on a new generation of turbulent dance.**

"There's a dishwasher, there's a dishwasher!" I called to Arty pulling at his shirtsleeve. "Come see. Come see."

The apartment we were looking at had a galley kitchen with all white cabinets and appliances. There was no window but that didn't matter—the built-in dishwasher was the "pièce de résistance." To me, this appliance was a sign of wealth. Hugging Arty, I asked, "Can we take this apartment? I love it."

While I basked in thoughts of our future in our new home, Arty spoke with the real estate agent and got the particulars. Concluding the conversation, he turned to me and said, "the apartment is ours. We can move in anytime."

And so we began our lives as husband and wife in a one bedroom apartment in Briarwood, Queens. We lived on the second floor. The living room was large with two picture windows. I hung crisp, sheer, white tieback curtains that added warmth and framed the view of a city street lined with maple trees. My cocoa brown, wingback sofa was big and overstuffed with two large throw pillows and a quilted throw resting on each arm. A multi-colored, oval hook rug lay in the center of the room beneath a cherry wood, rectangular coffee table. A country rocker sat in the corner near the window next to an antique butter churn lamp. The farm dining table was complemented by six bow-backed Windsor chairs. Judging by my choice of décor, it was clear that my mother's love of antiques and country living had rubbed off on me.

The country theme continued in the bedroom with our stained oak four poster bed as the focal point in the room. The fluffy comforter was soft and inviting, making it perfect for cuddling. There were night-stands on each side with lamps for reading, and our television sat on top of a four drawer dresser with a mirror hanging over a second dresser. My bedroom—our bedroom, I thought. This is where we would begin our family.

We settled into our new home fairly quickly. Arty was enjoying his work as a CPA in a midsize accounting firm where he was confident of growth—his goal was to become a partner. I was employed at a travel agency, and the combination of our two incomes made us financially stable. I traveled by subway from New York City to Queens and couldn't wait to get home and prepare dinner. I was playing house and enjoyed every moment.

- ♪ ♪ ♪ -

We loved spending time together. Nothing could separate us. But with the realization that Arty could be drafted into the army because of the Korean conflict, we knew we had to do something. He wasn't categorized 4F as his health was excellent and his educational deferment would end as of January 1960. Fatherhood was the only way he could get out of being drafted.

"I don't want you to go into the army. I don't want you to go away. Let's have a baby," I said, holding him close and nibbling at his ear.

"That's not a reason to have a baby," he said as he took me in his arms. "I won't be drafted tomorrow. We still have time to think about it."

I didn't know why, but secretly, I feared I'd have difficulty getting pregnant. I remember asking Arty if he would adopt if I couldn't conceive. I had two siblings, so I wanted to have at least three children for myself, and it didn't matter to me whether they were biological or adopted. When I was a child, I had yearned for recognition from my sister and brother, but because of the large gap in our ages, they wanted no part of a tag along kid sister. I wanted to fill that void in me with my own family.

It was mid December 1960. We continued our daily discussions on how Arty could avoid the draft.

"I'm going on a business trip next week. If you really want to have a baby, we'll try when I come home. I'll only be gone for five days," Arty told me.

That night we made love. Kissing my neck softly, his lips made their way to my ears and he whispered into them, "I love you," as if his heart were speaking aloud. We fell asleep in each other's arms.

I felt safe. When we awoke, we were still entwined. I didn't want to let go of him and started to cry as I watched him pack. I thought he was so handsome dressed in his dark blue suit and paisley tie. He wiped away my tears with his hankie.

"Don't cry," he said calmly. "We'll start a family when I return. My sister is staying with you this week, so you won't be too lonely."

He pulled me close. Embracing me, he kissed me passionately. Slowly releasing my hand, he said good-bye and left the house.

I cried hysterically as he closed the door. How could I live without him? Who would take care of me?

- ♪ ♪ ♪ -

January 20, 1961. It was a cold winter day with fresh snow on the ground. John F. Kennedy was being inaugurated as President of the United States. Arty and I watched the events unfold on television, and I was mesmerized as JFK took the oath of office. Jackie Kennedy was stunningly dressed in a royal blue suit with dark fur trim around her neck and a matching fur muff to warm her hands. The opening of JFK's inaugural address was compelling. His words still resonate for me.

"We observe today not a victory of party, but a celebration of freedom—symbolizing an end, as well as a beginning—signifying renewal, as well as change. For I have sworn before you and Almighty God the same solemn oath our forebears prescribed nearly a century and three quarters ago."

As I sat on our bed watching the inauguration, I craved something sweet, then immediately wanted something salty.

Unable to make up my mind, I told Arty, "I'm hungry." I'd heard that a pregnant woman craves pickles and ice cream, and my own cravings confirmed that myth. "Please get me a bowl of ice cream with pickles on the side...the baby needs to eat," I laughed.

Arty looked at me as if I were crazy, but quickly brought me the treats I'd craved—after all I was pregnant!

Mitchell David Levy was born on October 25, 1961. His ruddy complexion and puffy round face reminded me of my paternal grandfather after a night on the town. Mitchell had big blue eyes, a thin layer of dark brown hair, and a toothless smile that lit up my heart. I enjoyed everything about motherhood—his spitting up, changing dirty diapers, sleepless nights, the tears, and the laughter—it didn't matter as Mitchell was part of my soul. Arty and I were now a family.

We turned the bedroom into a nursery. The white crib and wicker dressing table were the centerpieces of the room. The scent in the room was a cross between Johnson's baby powder and Desitin. I couldn't get enough of the baby smell and took deep breaths every time I walked in the door. I'd hover over Mitchell's crib for hours and watch him smiling and kicking his little legs as his musical mobile circled above his head like a carousel. I was completely consumed by my son: his first words, his first steps, his first solid food, his discovery of the world.

My needs were totally fulfilled, or so I thought. I was only twenty when Mitchell was born. I was a child myself. How could

I know what my needs were? I fantasized that I was living in a "Cinderella" castle, with Arty as my Prince Charming, while my son scampered with laughter throughout our palace.

Remembering my childhood, I wanted more for my kids. I vowed to give them lots of love and grant them their every wish. I didn't want them to live in fear or struggle with anxieties. Unlike me, they'd grow up in a perfect world—a world where they'd feel superior and respected. But sometimes I would wonder: Was my hope for perfection reality or my dream? Was it for them or for me? Or was it my fear of my own past rising up? I mused about these feelings when I had some space for myself—especially when I drove.

Once, driving to my mom's house for a visit, I was listening to the car radio while Mitchell played with some Matchbox cars in the back seat—there were no seat belts or car seats in those years—and I'd glance at him every few minutes in the rear view mirror. I smiled joyfully as I watched him play—I was also three months pregnant.

"We interrupt this program to bring you a special report," the radio announcer said.

I turned up the volume. It was November 22, 1963.

"President Kennedy was shot in Dallas. President Kennedy was shot in Dallas while riding in his motorcade. I have no more information at this time." The reporter's voice was muffled as if he were crying.

I was in shock. I couldn't believe what I was hearing. This couldn't be. Kennedy and his wife were beloved by the world—they were Camelot.

I arrived at my mom's. She picked up my son, put her arm

around me, and kissed me on my forehead, as if to say everything would be OK.

"Let me make you and Mitchell something to eat. I'll heat up the chicken matzo ball soup, it has lots of noodles. Do you want a sandwich with the soup?" she asked.

Food was always her cure-all.

We sat in silence glued to the TV, and as we watched the news, my mother put her hand on my knee. The warmth of her palm penetrated my leg. They showed the horrific series of events as they occurred. The motorcade drove slowly with the President and his wife smiling and waving to the crowd, when suddenly a shot rang out. As he turned towards Jackie, he started to raise his hands and his expression changed dramatically—from a smile to astonishment. He slumped over, and a stunned Jackie Kennedy fell over her husband to shield him, her pink suit splattered with blood. My mom and I sat in horror. Not wanting to believe the President was dead, we hung onto every piece of news that was broadcasted. It seemed like hours before the Assistant Press Secretary, Malcom Kilduff, made the announcement.

"President John F. Kennedy died at approximately 1:00 p.m. Central Standard Time today here in Dallas. He died of a gunshot wound in the brain. I have no other details of the assassination."

The shocking news sunk into my brain along with the events that followed in the next three days. Seeing John John's salute as his father's funeral procession passed in front of him and Jackie Kennedy's control over her emotions were images permanently fixed in my mind forever.

I took the death of Kennedy personally. They had been a young family like me and Arty—full of life and just starting out. Jackie was only nine years older than me. Despite the fact that she was in the public eye and her children frolicked around the White House, she was a mother, like me. I idolized this couple, and felt her pain, as a wife and as a mother.

President Kennedy's assassination was the start of a tumultuous era which led to restlessness and discontent in the world.

- ♪ ♪ ♪ -

The following July 4th, we went to the beach with Arty's sister to watch the fireworks. Mitchell sat in awe as he watched the brilliant explosion of light fill the sky. Suddenly my stomach muscles tightened and I felt pressure in my lower abdomen—I was having my own fireworks—labor pains.

"Arty, I think I'm in labor," I said as my stomach tightened up. But the pains were not regular—I wasn't due for two weeks. Why was I having contractions?

Arty yanked me up from the blanket. "Let's go to the hospital now. I don't want the baby born on July 6th." He hesitated, "that's the anniversary of my mother's death."

Not knowing if it was false labor or the real thing, we asked his sister to babysit for Mitchell, and Arty rushed me off to the hospital. My labor was long and hard, and finally after being induced, my second son was born on July 5, 1964.

"It's a boy," I heard the nurse tell me as I slowly woke from the anesthesia. In those years they heavily sedated mothers whether they had a C-section or went into regular labor.

Not totally comprehending, I said, "A boy, no, it can't be a boy. We don't have a boy's name." I was sure I was having a girl—her name was to be Wendy Hope. I thought, I can't have a son without a name.

"Where's my husband?" I asked the nurse, in a panic, looking around the room.

"I'll get him," she said and handed me my newborn son. Suddenly my mood changed to euphoria. I rubbed my sleeping son's head gently and snuggled him closer to me in my arms. We must give him a good name, I thought, a meaningful name—he's so cute.

"Is everything alright?" Arty asked as he entered the room. "The nurse said you were in a panic."

"Look at your new son," I said. "He can't be nameless, we must give him a name now."

Arty sat on the bed, looked at me and then his son.

"Do you still want to name him in remembrance of your grandfather and mine? If so, we can call him William Henry?"

"No. Those are old men names. We can honor their memory by giving him their Hebrew names. I want a popular name, one that he can grow with."

Arty thought deeply and said, "I was listening to the Chicago White Sox game a few minutes ago. It was very exciting. Gary Peters pitched a no hitter—that's hard to do—it's a momentous accomplishment—our new son's birth is a momentous accomplishment! Let's name our son Gary Peter."

I wasn't surprised by Arty's suggestion since sometimes I thought baseball was his first love. Every year, the smells and sounds of spring would barely be in the air when Arty would tell me, "just one more month until spring training, only one month and the bats will start cracking." Perhaps he thought he was starting his own baseball team now that he had two sons.

"Gary Peter," I said looking at my son as he lay in my arms. "I like it, it's a strong name." Weighing in at 7 lbs 1 oz, our son had chubby cheeks, big brown eyes, and was 21 inches long. "You'll be an athlete for sure. Gary Peter," I said as joyous tears fell from my eyes.

- ♪ ♪ ♪ -

We moved from our apartment in Queens to a two-bedroom garden apartment in Oceanside, Long Island. The apartment was perfect for raising two kids. It was on the ground floor and the grassy courtyard was filled with lots of young children. Mitchell, three and a half years old, ran out the door holding his baseball bat with his glove dangling from his hand looking for friends. I sat on the front step and watched him play as I rocked Gary in his carriage. I met many other young mothers like myself, and we talked about our kids: what to do when your son has a tantrum or doesn't share his toys, how to instill good eating habits, etc. The topics got more intimate when we discussed the needs of our husbands and how we balanced or didn't balance time between our kids and our mates. The subject got even more heated when we discussed sex. One friend said sarcastically, "Sex! What's that? It's been so long, I can't remember anymore. I have no desire. I am so tired by the time I get the kids to sleep, I pass out before my husband comes to bed."

Another said, "I can't think about sex when my day is focused around changing diapers, bathing the kids, and doing laundry. My husband doesn't ask anymore—he just gives me a kiss goodnight."

Just like my friends, my attention to my husband and his desires was greatly reduced. I gave my kids 100% of my energy and time. Arty understood, so I thought—but in retrospect, did he? He started coming home later and many evenings got home after the kids were in bed. We ate dinner together less and less often. When he did get home early, the first thing he did was pour himself a drink. He was telling me something, but I wasn't listening. I was oblivious, caught up in a dream world.

Our apartment was known as a railroad flat. There was a long hall with the bedrooms connecting to one another in a straight line—just like cars on a train. The close proximity of our bedrooms made me feel secure, since I was able to hear my sons' laughter and their cries. Their room was painted blue, and I hung a border depicting baseball, basketball, and football on the wall. A light blue shag carpet and the many stuffed animals that lined the wall next to the crib, and the big red fire truck and rocking horse next to Mitchell's bed all added to the warmth of the room. The toy chest overflowed with toys for both boys. Their bedroom was a safe haven filled with happiness.

"Mitchell, let your brother play ball too," I shouted from the front door of our new home. We moved from our garden apartment when Gary turned one. The new house was in the center of a cul-de-sac in a new development in Oceanside, N.Y. There were twenty other homes that made up this neighborhood of young families.

I was the perfect mom. As class mother for the nursery school, I went on all the field trips, volunteered as a teacher's aid and took the kids to their friends' houses to play. I did everything for our kids. I thought I was happy—yet I had no idea I was running from myself. I didn't realize external forces were pulling at me—my husband, my kids, my friends, my family. When did I have time for myself? What did I want?

I had gotten married so young; I thought that was going to fulfill me. My generation followed the idealized mold of the 1950s which meant that a woman would go from getting married right out of high school to immediately raising a family. It wasn't until I developed a close friendship with my neighbor, Annie, that I realized I had missed out on a lot. I wasn't conscious of it, but her wild stories opened my eyes. Annie had an engaging personality and a curvy figure like a Playboy Bunny. She also was a pothead and taught me how to smoke.

"C'mon take a toke. Drag on the joint, breathe in, hold it, and exhale. No worries, I have quality weed. As long as it has the scent of pine trees it's good pot. Go ahead. Take a whiff."

I was hesitant, but Annie looked so relaxed and happy. I put my fear aside and took the joint. Inhaling, I held my breath—exhaled and looked up at her lighting fixture. It was an ox yoke with one bow encompassing a round amber globe. I stared at the light waiting to feel the effect of the pot.

"What's taking so long?" I asked. "I don't feel any different."

"Here take another toke."

It was difficult to describe what I felt, but immediately after my second toke, I began to feel differently. Then, suddenly, I got the munchies. There was a big bowl of popcorn in the middle of the table and I grabbed a handful. Annie chuckled as she joined me. Looking around at the ox yoke lighting fixture in her kitchen, I felt as if I was sitting in a saloon waiting for Billy the Kid. We began to laugh hysterically, I'm not sure why, but everything seemed funny. If feeling happy and content meant I was stoned—I guess I was stoned. It seemed like I was there for hours, gabbing about our experiences with old boyfriends, comparing notes.

Suddenly the front door opened and Arty walked in.

"What are you doing? I've been home for an hour waiting for you."

Looking around the room, he sniffed the marijuana, waved his hand in disgust, and left.

- ♪ ♪ ♪ -

JFK's assassination changed the mood of the country, and the atmosphere of the 1960s was unsettled. It was the decade of flower power, hippies, the anti war movement, bell bottoms, drugs, free love, peace marches, and Woodstock. People were rebellious. They were running scared and searching for answers to happiness through alcohol and drugs. Arty and I got caught up in the chaos too. We gave ourselves carte blanche to engage in wild parties where the booze flowed freely and potheads shared bongs. My kids were still my top priority while Arty continued to wait on the sidelines. I started to indulge in wild behavior. I began to drink martinis, smoke more pot, and become more flirtatious. Arty followed my lead...or was I following his? We were escaping both the country's woes and the confines of our family. Subconsciously, I must have known that I wanted more.

The country was still healing from JFK's assassination when once again we were stunned by another murder. On April 4, 1968, Civil Rights Leader, Martin Luther King was assassinated on a hotel balcony in Memphis. President Lyndon Johnson said he was "shocked and saddened" by Dr. King's death.

"I ask every citizen to reject the blind violence that has taken Dr. King who lived by non-violence."

Riots flared. The world continued to fall apart. Still raw from Dr. King's death, we were shocked yet again on June 5, 1968 when Senator Robert F. Kennedy, who was campaigning for the Democratic Presidential nomination, was shot leaving the ballroom of the Embassy Hotel in Los Angeles. He had been speaking about overcoming racial divisions and the end of the unpopular Vietnam War. Press Secretary Fred Mankiewicz interrupted the airways.

"Senator Robert Francis Kennedy died at 1:44 a.m. today... he was forty-two years old."

We all mourned. The country's climate was bitter.

Arty and I gathered around the television set in our house with friends as we watched the frightening events. The shootings were just two months apart. The picture of Dr. King's gunshot to his neck was still fresh in our minds when we watched an assailant come up on Senator Kennedy and gun him down while surrounded by Secret

Service. We all sat in disbelief. "What is this world coming to?" a friend asked as he sipped his martini. "How could someone get past the security?"

"Does anyone want another martini?" Arty asked. "I'm making a new batch."

Our escape through drinking and drugs helped rub out the reality of the unsettled world. This behavior also reflected the restlessness of our marriage. One minute Arty would be resentful of my friendship with Annie—the next minute we'd jump into bed and have fiery sex. Our marriage and its patterns continued to be a product of the times, however I wouldn't realize this pattern until years later.

It was 1968. I was twenty-seven. Mitchell was seven and Gary was turning five. With the kids in school all day the house felt empty. Impulsively I said to Arty, "I want to have another baby. Mitchell and Gary are big boys—it would be fun to have a little one around again." I think I said it because I thought that having another child would fill the void in me.

Surprisingly, Arty said, "OK." I was amazed that he didn't resist me, but figured that perhaps he still wanted to fulfill his dream of having his own baseball team.

In July of 1968, Arty and I made passionate love while on vacation in the Amish Country with our boys. We had come back to the hotel room after a romantic dinner. Arty and I got into our bed and watched our boys sleeping peacefully. Smiling at our creations, we kissed. I felt closer to Arty at that moment than I had felt in a long time, and Kenneth Scott Levy was the result of our passion. He was born on March 13, 1969.

Kenny had blond hair and his eyes were deep blue like Mitchell's, but he was tiny, the littlest of my boys, weighing in at a little more than six pounds. He even lost weight while he was in the hospital. He looked like a small toy doll—a cherub—and Arty nicknamed him "Toy Boy." At three weeks he developed an itchy, bumpy, scaly rash on his face; it was eczema, a mild topical skin rash. Even though it wasn't serious, it pained me to watch his little hands scratch the rash.

Enjoying my infant son, I went back to playing house—only things had changed. Once again it was hard to regain the intimacy between Arty and me. Like before, I continued to put the needs of my children before Arty's needs. I decided to breast-feed, since bottle-feeding was becoming less popular due to media reports that canned formulas were harder for the baby to digest. I remember calling the La Leche League. I was concerned that Kenny wasn't getting enough milk, but they told me to let the baby nurse five to ten minutes on each breast, and the number of wet diapers—five to eight in a 24 hour period—would assure me that the baby was getting enough nourishment. I was at peace when I'd rock him in my country rocker and watch him fall asleep in my arms. I nursed Kenny for six months, and it was one of the most gratifying experiences I'd ever had.

I wondered if Arty was jealous of my breast-feeding. He never stopped me, but our sex life was limited during this time. I believe he feared my breast milk would flow while making love. He spent his time playing ball with Mitchell and Gary. He was Mitchell's Little League coach, and when he wasn't working, he scheduled baseball practices and games. I was happy to see him become a real family man. Our out-of-control parties with heavy drinking and pot smoking had been put on hold for the moment—but we continued a nightly cocktail.

After six months of breast-feeding, I craved freedom from the routine of motherhood. I hired a full time nanny and went back to work part time at a local travel agency. Working as a travel agent gave me opportunities to travel. I remember being afraid to take a familiarization trip to Myrtle Beach, South Carolina and I looked to Arty for reassurance. I would be on my own, Arty wouldn't be there to take care of me—would I be able to make decisions for myself? Would I make friends? Would I be comfortable sleeping alone? My repressed feelings surfaced—the little girl inside appeared. After a month's discussion, Arty was annoyed with my nervous chatter. He raised his arms and shouted, "For Christ's sake, grow up!"

I boarded the plane the following week.

It was during this trip that I had an affair. I remember thinking—was this real or a fantasy as I lay in bed next to this stranger. Was it lust or love? I was emotionally starved, only I didn't know it. I allowed myself to give into the romantic folly and enjoy this idealistic adventure. Consumed with guilt when I returned home, I tried to justify my actions. Was it because I married so young? What happened to the butterflies in my tummy when Arty entered the room? Why did the sizzle of our marriage dissipate? Was Arty not living up to my expectations? When we first married our focus was on each other. With the birth of each child, the dynamics of our relationship changed with more of my attention going to the kids and Arty's to building his career. Without realizing it, we were growing apart. I didn't want to hurt Arty, yet I was unable to let go. I continued the affair for three months. The world was in a state of confusion and so was I.

On Valentine's Day, Arty took me to a romantic restaurant in New York City, called A Quiet Little Table In The Corner, to celebrate. Surprised by his invite I wondered if he suspected something. I put the thought out of my head as I put on my makeup and blew dry my hair. I pulled down my hem to just above my knees and stepped into my new red pumps. Looking good, I thought, as I stood in front of my full length mirror.

We arrived at the restaurant and the hostess took us to our quiet little table in the corner. The red and black flocked wallpaper created a romantic yet sexy ambience, the lights were dimly lit, and candles and bud vases filled with a single rose sat on each table. We sat holding hands as we ordered drinks. "Cheers," we said as we clicked our glasses. Our conversation revolved around the kids at first, but as the alcohol loosened our tongues, the talk became more intense.

"Rosann," he started holding tightly onto my hand. "I don't know how to say this to you, but I know you are having an affair. Your behavior has changed over the past few months. Our sex life has lost some of its passion and sometimes I smell a scent of a man's cologne when I kiss you hello. You run to Annie's whenever you get a chance and when we are home alone, you are not attentive." He paused, took a deep breath, and loosened his grip on my hand. "I don't know for sure what is going on, or why, but I surmise the familiarization trip had something to do with it." He reached out and held my face in his hands and said, "I don't want to know who it is, why you are doing this, or how often; I am only asking you to stop and come home. I love you and want you back!" My mouth fell open and I began to cry softly. He wiped my tears.

I looked at him with shameful teary eyes, yet I felt relieved. It was as if I wanted him to know so the guilt would leave me and I would be free. My voice was barely audible as I struggled to get my words out. "Can you forgive me?" He took me in his arms and hugged me. That night we began to reacquaint as we sat at our quiet little table in the corner.

- ♪ ♪ ♪ -

Anti-Vietnam War rallies continued with activists protesting and burning the American flag. As the president of a group called Women Strike for Peace, my sister aggressively campaigned against the war. Arty and I joined her efforts. I believed that making our voices heard would someday protect my sons from going to war.

We attended a rally with Congresswoman Bella Abzug and chained ourselves to the fence at the White House. We marched in a Memorial Day Parade, holding posters that said "Make Love Not War." The hostile crowd threw eggs, and one hit Arty on his forehead. I started to run away, pulling Arty with me. The police arrested Arty, and although he escaped going to jail, he was cited for creating a public disturbance.

Our anti-war activities bonded us and sparked a new desire for intimacy—we made love not war.

Anti-war rallies continued throughout the summer. Uncertainty lingered, defiance ruled. Yet out of this counterculture a legendary festival was born—Woodstock where thirty-two of the best musicians came together for a three day weekend in August to spread peace and love through their music. Over 400,000 people attended this historic rock concert, including anti-war protestors, black militants, gays, lesbians, anti-gays, anti-government advocates, pro-government advocates, and some who came just to hear the music. This non-violent festival is remembered as one of the greatest happenings in the history of music and defined a generation—my generation.

- ♪ ♪ ♪ -

"Arty," I shouted with excitement one day while opening the mail. "Look magazine has a picture of a baby on the cover and the headline reads; 'Choose Your Baby's Sex'!"

It was April 1970. I wanted Kenny to have a friend. He was home alone with our nanny most of the time—and deep inside I wanted a girl. It was my mother's wish, too.

"Read the article. We can meet with the doctor and try. If it really works, we'll have a daughter," I said.

"No more kids," he said. "Don't we have enough? More kids means we'll have to spend more money, we'll have less freedom, more work. Why would I want to have more?"

We never met with the doctor—we never discussed it again. Instead, I got pregnant.

"It's a girl, it's a girl," Arty shouted ecstatically as he entered my hospital room. Tracy Elizabeth Levy was born December 21, 1970.

"We have a daughter," I said. "Everything will be pink—her room, her blankets, her dresses, the bows for her hair." I laughed as I looked at her sleeping in her crib—she had only a few wisps of brown hair, but I would find a strand for a pink bow.

She slept in a bassinet next to our bed with her pink blanket for the lining. When I woke to nurse her, I smiled—pink was my favorite color. I felt as if my dreams were fulfilled. But Arty was restless and wanted me back as his playmate. Subconsciously I struggled with his unrest as I did with my own.

One evening, when I had just finished nursing Tracy and put her back in her bassinet, Arty confronted me.

"I'm going to the Catskill Mountains this weekend with our friends, and I want you to come with me."

"How can I leave Tracy, she's still an infant?" I asked. "I won't stop you from going, but I can't go." This time, for the first time, I wasn't afraid to be without Arty. I was secure in my own home and didn't need Arty as my crutch.

I struggled with my quick decision, convincing myself there was no way I could leave my baby.

My nanny overheard our conversation and took me aside.

"Mrs. Levy, I don't mean to interfere, but you need to go with your husband. Your baby is in good hands with me. You must go," she said shaking her finger at me. I was surprised at her insistent words, but listened to what she said. I awoke the next morning and packed.

Arty grabbed the suitcase and then took my hand. "Let's go," he said.

I kissed the kids goodbye and we left. I nursed Tracy for only six weeks.

Going to the mountains proved to be the right decision, because I noticed that another woman who I thought was my friend was hitting on Arty. His body language at the bar showed me his vulnerability as he put his arm around her. I was seething as I ordered a glass of wine but smiled and joined in on the conversation. When she excused herself, I followed her to the ladies' room. Racing in front of her, I didn't let her enter the stall and pushed her to the sink. I was trying to decide between punching her or spitting in her face but managed to control myself. In a voice filled with venom, I said, "You stay away from my husband! He's off limits." I stormed out shaking and immediately went to Arty's side as if I were his armed guard.

Arty and I made love that night as if nothing had happened. I thought to myself that our marriage was like riding the Coney Island Cyclone—we weathered the storms through bad times and good times and wound up sharing intense excitement.

One week later, Arty announced, "I bought a sports car—it's a red Triumph convertible."

"We have two cars, why do we need another?" I said only half listening. Kissing him quickly on his cheek as I shoved the spoon of applesauce in Tracy's mouth, I thought that he must be having a mid-life crisis.

"If you can have four children, I can have a sports car. You can't argue with me. I've given in a deposit and I'm getting it next week. If you can tear yourself away from the kids, I might give you a ride," he said.

I ran out the front door as Arty drove the car into our driveway. Mitchell, Gary, and I crowded around it. It looked like a wind up toy, but as he revved up the engine, Arty's face lit up like a little kid. The boys shouted in unison, "Take me for a ride, take me for a ride!"

"Hop in," he said, and after they did the car sped away. I was conflicted as I watched the car disappear down the street. What did this car represent? What did Arty really want? What did I want? Although we lived under the same roof, we led separate lives.

It was 1973. I was in my thirties. We were getting older, and our age dictated our actions. I hung onto my hippie ideals but wanted more. I yearned to be accepted by the mainstream. Having outgrown our first home we bought a bigger house in a more prestigious community. Our new home was an eighty-year-old center hall Dutch Colonial with three floors and six bedrooms—one for each kid and one for our full time nanny. It was a beautiful old house with lots of charm—a symbol of wealth, power, and a higher social standing. We were stepping up; climbing the status ladder. Our new home represented the elite; I thought this would make us happy.

"Arty, a new tennis club opened down near the beach," I said one evening after we'd moved in. "Let's join. We can take lessons, play in tournaments, and even give the kids lessons."

I was seeking ways to keep myself feeling young. Tennis was the most respected sport and in its height of popularity. I wanted to be a part of it; Billie Jean King had just beat Bobby Riggs in a match known as the "Battle of the Sexes," and I wanted to be like Billie Jean King. My tennis game would emulate hers—serve and volley.

I loved being on center court.

Our lives revolved around tennis for the next five years. We made many new friends. Everyone carried their little black books making tennis dates with whomever they deemed "A" players. If you didn't fit their description, you weren't asked to play. Thank goodness, I was considered an "A" player. Arty made his way too and won the Juvenile Diabetes men's doubles tournament every year. We were accepted into the "in crowd" which made me feel important.

Arty and I were a team on the courts—but tennis was only a Band-aid on our vulnerable, roller coaster, Lindy Hop dance of a marriage.

- ♪ ♪ ♪ -

Blues Dancing

Blues dancing evolved from Africa
and is tied to Blues music. A few of the Blues dances
are known as the Cake Walk and the Fishtail.
Blues dance demonstrates the passion
of a whole range of emotions—
from sadness to joy—not just sensuality.

A Cold Wet Towel

Many features of Blues dancing would tap into the intensity of my emotions and ignite a tension as I danced to the blues in my own world.

I heard Arty's voice. "I want to see my wife; I want to see my wife NOW!"

As I lay on the stretcher in the emergency room of the hospital, I wanted him by my side but I couldn't speak. I heard the doctors say, "Her blood pressure is falling rapidly, shoot her up with adrenaline, then Benadryl quickly, or we'll lose her."

Through my haze, I didn't grasp the seriousness of my allergic reaction. I was in shock, anaphylactic shock.

I had always loved seafood, especially shellfish. But growing up in a kosher home, I was never allowed to eat it. Early on in our marriage, during a weekend trip to Atlantic City, Arty introduced me to my first bucket of steamers. Initially afraid to touch them, I opened the clamshell with a fork and dipped the clam belly into the melted butter. The butter disguised the taste making my sampling tolerable, but by the time we finished the bucket, I was smacking my lips in delight.

"Can we order more?" I asked.

He laughed and said, "No, now you're going to try lobster."

Before the trip to Atlantic City, I had enjoyed chicken—especially gnawing on the leg bones drawing out the marrow and cleaning the rib bones dry. Lobster replaced that first love. Sucking the sweet juices from the lobster's scrawny legs, cracking the claws with a nutcracker, and pulling out the succulent meat was a real treat.

During the summer of 1970, I was pregnant with Tracy, but I still favored the fish at Jimmy's Seafood Restaurant. Arty, sensitive to my needs and cravings, took me there frequently. The red and white checked tablecloths, fresh parmesan cheese, bottles of Chianti hanging from the beamed ceiling, homemade pasta, and fresh fish made me feel as if I were in dining in a small Italian village in Tuscany. The restaurant's specialty was linguine with white clam sauce bathed in garlic and oil. I can still remember the smell of the garlic and the taste of the Italian spices as I put the fork to my mouth. "Mangia, Mangia," the waiter said as he served us our food.

My palms began to itch shortly after we returned home from dinner. I looked at the red blotches and couldn't stop scratching. I called my obstetrician. After I explained my symptoms, he said, "It sounds as if you are having an allergic reaction to the clams. Take a cool bath and two antihistamines every four hours until the hives subside."

His diagnosis was correct and his prescription worked

quickly.

I never considered the full ramifications of this allergic reaction. I continued to eat clams and shellfish for nine years. Actifed and cool baths always made me feel better.

In March 1978, the price of beef had skyrocketed, and for one month I boycotted buying meat. In protest I decided to make a different fish dish every night. In preparation for dinner one evening, I went to my library of cookbooks resting on the kitchen counter and reached for my cooking bible, *The New York Times Cookbook*. As I leafed through the pages for ideas, I smiled as I noticed that some of the pages were smudged with the residue of spices from previously used recipes.

I decided that my menu for dinner would comprise of sautéed soft-shell crab, mixed green salad, steamed broccoli, and carrots. As I flipped the crabs in the frying pan, I sprinkled them with fresh minced parsley, onion, and crushed garlic. The smell of the fresh herbs combined with the shellfish permeated throughout the kitchen. My taste buds came alive and my mouth began to water.

When Arty got home, he noticed the red tablecloth, cloth napkins, the lights dimmed with candles lighting the room, and said, "What's the occasion?"

"I went to the Lobster Shanty today and bought fresh soft-shell crabs, your favorite. Joe told me they just came in off the boat and would make for a special dinner. I couldn't resist."

Arty walked to the stove, took the lid off the pan, and inhaled the aroma of the fresh seafood. He looked at me and smiled.

"Open a bottle of good red wine," I said. "I'll get the kids to bed and we can sit and enjoy a romantic dinner."

It was 8:30 p.m. by the time we first sat down to enjoy the fruits of my labor. Arty poured the wine. We clicked glasses.

"Cheers."

I watched as Arty took his first bite, waiting for his critique. Arty looked at me, paused as he slowly chewed his food, and finally said, "Delicious, I couldn't have done it any better myself!"

Arty loved to cook too, and sometimes we'd have cook-off competitions, but this night he gave me all the credit. It was a most enjoyable dinner; we had good food, good conversation, and most important of all, we appreciated each other.

At 9:30 p.m., while I was finishing the dishes, I suddenly felt nauseous. I walked to the living room, where Arty sat reading a book. Within minutes I felt my stomach begin to spasm. Rubbing my stomach, I said in a worried voice, "Arty, I don't feel well; my stomach aches and it's not a usual ache."

The sudden muscle contractions of my stomach were intense. Breaking out in a cold sweat, I doubled over in fright.

Arty followed me as I ran upstairs to the bathroom. I looked in the mirror and my color scared me. I was pale, almost green. There were red welts on my neck and my pupils were dilated. Looking for a quick fix, I reached for the Actifed, popped two in my mouth, and drew a cool bath. My breathing grew short. This was not my usual allergic reaction to fish. I began to panic.

"Arty, hand me a wet cool towel. I feel as if I am burning up, my throat is closing, I can't breathe."

Arty picked up the phone and said, "I'm calling the doctor." In a fog, I heard his concerned voice saying to the answering service, "My wife is having trouble breathing; her throat is closing."

A Cold Wet Towel

All I remember is that the doctor told Arty to rush me to the hospital and said he would meet us there. Arty called our neighbor to stay with the kids. I leaned heavily on him, dragging my cold, wet towel as he took me to the car. I don't recall how long it took to get the hospital, but I remember Arty speeding and running lights. I had the window fully open to give me air, thinking this would help me breathe. The towel was like a security blanket, and I kept it across my forehead to keep me cool.

I was delirious when I arrived at the hospital, and Arty had to carry me into the emergency waiting room. I clung to the towel, which was no longer cold, as Arty laid me across some chairs.

As two men, wearing green scrubs, transferred me to a stretcher and wheeled me into the emergency room, my head felt as if it were exploding and separating from my body. I didn't know what was happening. I couldn't understand why I wasn't able to speak. Was I hallucinating? I had no control of my body, it was shutting down, as if it was on automatic pilot, yet nothing hurt.

Barely conscious, I heard my husband's voice.

My stomach convulsed with involuntary spasms causing me to violently heave. In an instant, everything I had eaten was expelled from my gut, and I projectile vomited into a metal pan placed just below my chin. There it was: my entire dinner of soft-shell crabs, claws barely digested. My exposed chest and abdomen were covered with large red blotches, and my nails near the cuticles were a very dark blue-purple.

Blue fingernails! Am I going to die?

I remembered before I gave birth to each child, the doctor told me I had to remove my nail-polish.

"I must be able to see the color of your skin beneath your nails," he said. "Blue fingernails are a sign of low blood pressure and low oxygen in the blood stream."

Arty was at my side holding my hand. I told him to look at my nails. Hooked up to an IV, my arm encased with a blood pressure sleeve, the doctor looked at me and spoke softly.

"Take it easy. You had an allergic reaction to the crabs and went into anaphylactic shock. Anaphylactic shock," he explained to us, "is a severe life threatening allergic reaction causing rapid closing of the air passage from the mouth, throat, and nose to the lungs within minutes of its onset. Symptoms include fainting, itching, swelling of the throat, and a sudden decline in blood pressure. We thought we were going to lose you," the doctor told me. "We're going to keep you here for a few hours until your pressure stabilizes."

I fell asleep.

- ♪ ♪ ♪ -

That life-threatening crisis would change my life forever. Thinking back to the turn of events that night in the hospital, I remember wanting to speak but not being able to speak. I could hear my husband's voice and the voice of the doctors, but I couldn't acknowledge anyone or anything. I just lay there; helpless.

For the first time, I had to face up to my own mortality.

I met with the doctor the day after returning home from the

hospital. He discussed the events from the night before. Explaining the seriousness of anaphylactic shock, he told me it's not to be taken lightly.

"You almost died," he said. "If your husband didn't get you to the hospital as quickly as he did, we would have lost you. You are never to eat shellfish again. Don't even bring it into the house, and for a few months, don't dine at any seafood restaurants since sometimes the smell of fish can trigger an attack."

He also advised that I carry a syringe of epinephrine with me at all times. He explained that it was a form of adrenaline that relaxes the airways, and that I should be prepared to administer a shot if I ever felt an attack coming on.

The words "I almost died," echoed over and over again as I left his office. Death or any related words to death were not in my vocabulary. Death was what happened to the elderly and very sick. It couldn't happen to me. I made a commitment to myself not to eat shellfish, or any fish for that matter, from then on, but did I really want to carry around an epinephrine syringe? No, I thought to myself, this couldn't happen again. I was a good person—God would protect me.

My hives returned mid-spring. Arty and I had decided to go to a tennis camp run by a world famous tennis coach. The getaway was held at a college in upstate New York. We slept in dorms, arose at the crack of dawn, and started our day with tennis drills. These drills trained us on net shots, overheads, smart placement of ground strokes, and my favorite, putting away the overheads. The training was intense. The morning sun blazed onto the courts, and as the temperature rose, perspiration covered my body. Aware that I was beginning to overheat, I poured cups of cold water over my head. Observing the cool liquid dribble down my body, my eyes opened wider as I saw red welts break out on my ankles. Concerned the swelling would travel to my throat, I immediately ran off the court and into a cold shower. Anxious about what was happening to me, I started to shiver. Automatically, I glanced at my nails to be sure that they weren't turning blue. Racked with fear, not comprehending what was happening, I prayed.

"Dear God, please watch over me. I'll be good..."

The hives reappeared periodically for about a month, and I couldn't understand why. I had stopped eating shellfish. I didn't even eat tuna fish, fresh or canned, and I had also eliminated smoked salmon, which to me was "Jewish soul food," a favorite Sunday morning treat, sandwiched between bagels and smothered with cream cheese.

Since I was in complete denial of my condition, I followed my usual remedy—continuing to take cool baths or showers and popping Actifed tablets hoping the red blotches would disappear completely. Disgusted with the constant reoccurrence, I finally decided to consult with a doctor.

"What's causing my hives now?" I asked the allergist.

The short, balding man pricked my skin with a needle and said, "Hives can come from many things, that's why we're testing. Keep a daily diary of everything you eat and drink as well as your activities. It will help determine my diagnosis."

After a month of testing for a variety of foods, with the exception of fish, my doctor didn't find any food allergies, but instead believed that my high body temperature had been the culprit. He told me to cool it on the tennis court, to avoid playing in the heat of the day, and warned me to cut out my daily martinis.

The tennis I could deal with but the martini-less nights would be devastating—how could I possibly eliminate them? Sipping the smooth, syrupy vodka martinis with Arty before dinner was our sacred ritual; it was our quality time together and the slight buzz took the edge off the stress of our days and loosened our tongues for open communication. I couldn't give it up. Trying to think of a quick fix, I impulsively asked, "Can I drink wine?"

"If you must," was his response.

First shellfish and now my martini, what would I have to give up next?

A few days later, I felt on edge as we dined with friends at a local steak house. The flavorful steaks, accompanied by gorgonzola dressing on chopped lettuce and tomatoes, was a favorite meal of mine, and I always looked forward to dining there. I couldn't explain my edginess; perhaps it was because I couldn't have my martini, I thought. I tried to engage in conversation, but my mind kept wandering. I couldn't focus. I wondered if my friends were suspicious of my strange behavior—not being able to sit still and constantly running to the ladies' room where I'd splash water on my face to cool down my body temperature. Halfway through the dinner, unbearable fear came upon me. I leaned toward Arty and whispered, "My ears feel as if they are going to explode the pressure, please take me home."

Arty felt my forehead and calmly said, "Your head feels cool, you look fine, your color is good, it's nothing. Stop worrying and finish your dinner."

"No, no, I can't stand it," I said, my voice a bit louder. "Please take me home now."

Apologizing, Arty left money for our share of the meal, and we left for home.

As I lay on my side in our bed, Arty handed me a cool wet towel, which I thought of as my security blanket. I kept rotating the towel from ear to ear, hoping it would make the pressure I felt within subside.

This night became one of many, with Arty routinely taking me home from our dinner dates and bringing me my towel as I lay on the bed. I wasn't aware that anxiety was taking possession of my body. Fearing my throat would once again swell and my stomach would ache, I felt out of control. My nerves shattered, I questioned myself. Was I imagining the intense explosion in my head? Was it some lasting psychological shift or was I just experiencing a difficult time in my life? Was there some lesson I had to learn before the fear and symptoms would stop?

Whatever was happening, real or imaginary, I began to distrust friends, neighbors, and even some family members. Paranoia set in. I grew sensitive to negative comments or perceived unfriendly gestures. Insecurities from my childhood started rising up, and I could sense my father's rigidity and strict discipline all around me. His voice reverberated in my head, saying, "any dummy can do it," insinuating my incapability and incompetence. He was the authority figure, and if he implied I wasn't worthy—I wasn't. Every day and soon every hour, I would shake my head vigorously, trying to rid myself of his words. I felt trapped and I began to speak to God, repeating over and over, "I'm not a bad person, I'm not bad. Please don't punish me..."

It was early June 1978. My tennis club had opened for the summer season and I had games scheduled every day. Seeking ways to protect myself from the people playing tennis who I sensed would be verbally threatening, I asked a doctor friend of mine to prescribe me Valium, which I heard could quell anxiety. The prescription did work wonders for awhile. Whenever I felt insecure, I'd pop the little yellow pill into my mouth as if it were my crutch.

Playing in the finals of a mixed doubles tennis tournament on the July 4th holiday weekend, I took my Valium before heading to the courts. Feeling tranquil, I greeted my partner, shook hands with the opposing team, and started to hit balls in our warm up. Shortly after the game began, it was my turn to serve. Tossing the ball in the air, I brought my racquet back. Looking for an ace; I flexed my wrist, came down hard, and missed hitting the ball. Horrified that I had failed my partner, the racquet fell limply in my hand, my feet slipped from under me, my butt landed on the grainy har-tru with pieces of green grit left sticking to the back of my thighs. My head was heavy and felt detached from my body. Was the Valium not working? Had I overdosed? Was I suddenly immune to its effects? I didn't understand. When I looked up at my partner, his face was blurry. He pulled me up and brought me to a bench. I requested my cold wet towel and placed it on my head. Again, I felt the same explosive feeling within that continued to rule me.

After that incident, I lost trust in the little yellow pills, and

I started to use my swimming pool as their replacement. An 18 x 36 L-shape with a vinyl liner made to look like mosaic tiles, our pool was the focal point in the backyard. I was confident the cool calm water wouldn't let me down like the Valium had; it remained a consistent healer. There were days after playing tennis for hours in the heat, I'd long for that invigorating fix and rush home to jump into the pool still wearing my tennis clothes, taking off my sneakers and discarding them to the side of the pool. Swimming never failed to cool me down and settle my nerves.

I also made it a habit to swim every night before I went to bed. My dog, a Saint Bernard named Maggie who never left my side, sat on the edge of the pool as if she were my lifeguard. Night after night, stars lit up the dark sky as I lay on a raft wishing my demons would go away. Closing my eyes I saw multi-colored aliens, red orange, blue, and yellow, circling my head ready to pounce—distorted mutants with pointy ears and piercing green eyes waiting to puncture my scalp. I silently cried out to God seeking protection. As always, the coolness of the water settled me, and with Maggie at my side, I felt secure. I felt certain that God must have heard my request.

But the demons didn't leave.

- ♪ ♪ ♪ -

The weekend following the July 4th holiday and my breakdown on the courts, I had a disturbing phone conversation with Arty's aunt. She was accusatory and judged me because I didn't agree with her about some family politics with her brother, Arty's father. I felt personally assaulted and this activated another anxiety attack.

Sensing my head begin to swell, I ran out to the pool and jumped in, thinking it would cool me down. As the water splashed over my head, I felt as if I couldn't stay afloat and began to sink. Panicking, I thought, "I'm going to drown." I struggled to reach for the side of the pool. I was powerless as my arms flailed and moved violently in the water. Gagging on the taste of chlorine, I fought desperately until I finally reached the edge, which in reality was only a foot away. It took all my strength to pull myself out. Shaking, I immediately lay down on a chaise and wrapped myself in a towel.

I don't remember going to bed, but when I awoke the next morning, my body was curled up in a fetal position, with my knees crunched against my chest. Clutching the blanket, I pulled it up to my chin hoping it would protect me from myself. Panic spiraled through my body. Up until that moment, I had avoided neighbors and friends; now I feared going to my kitchen. I envisioned struggling with a knife pointed at my gut. I also imagined slashing my wrists with razor blades, making the bathroom off limits to me too. Other thoughts, like running in front of a bus or jumping off a bridge, crossed my mind; anything that might help put me out of my misery. But at the moment holding a knife in my hand was high on my list.

By this time Arty was used to my panic attacks. He stood over me and shook his head, as if to say "no, not again." Not realizing this time was different, he raised his arms in disgust and shouted, "For God's sake, go see a shrink!" He closed the blinds and left for work. I looked at my duvet cover. It was pale yellow. I imagined my face was that same color. Scanning the room, I noticed the walls were also pale yellow; everything blended, my duvet, the walls, and my face.

The room grew bigger as my eyes inspected each corner, noticing the chipped paint, cracks in the crown molding, the shaggy ivory carpet with coffee stains—everything stood out. I didn't understand what was happening.

Noticing Maggie lying at the foot of the bed, I called out for her. She came and sat next to me, resting her chin on the mattress. She was so beautiful, with black raccoon circles highlighting her kind eyes, her damp warm nose snuggled toward my face. Her nearness was comforting and gave me the strength to drag myself out of bed. Sitting up slowly, I grabbed Maggie's collar as if she were my guide dog. Cautiously walking to the closet, I reached for my robe and wrapped it around my body. I slowly made my way to the stairs.

With Maggie at my side, I gripped the banister tightly. Planting one foot at a time firmly on each step, I tried to balance. I was shaky; it took all my inner strength to keep me from falling. My chest pounded with palpitations, as I gulped for air, trying desperately to fight off suicidal thoughts. I wondered why I was going downstairs. Was I heading toward the kitchen? Did I really want to kill myself? Was I going to open the kitchen drawer? My mind was telling me to do so, but my body fought back. Why? Why? I kept asking myself as I continued my way down the stairs very slowly, doubting my every thought; my every move. I didn't understand what was happening to me. As I took the last step, relief took over and I began to breathe a bit more freely. Looking back up the stairs, I took a little bit of pleasure in my sense of accomplishment. It was as if I had just climbed down Mt. Everest! For a brief, glorious instant the panic left me.

Looking down our wood-paneled hall to the kitchen, I

hesitated. Did I really want to go there? I could go back upstairs where I would be safe. Fighting with myself, the kitchen won out and I forged forward. The knives were in the drawer on my left as I entered. Taking small steps, I inched myself to the right, opened the cabinet, reached for a glass, and turned on the kitchen faucet. I filled my glass, feeling beads of perspiration form on my brow. Staring at the closed drawer, I slowly sipped the water. Maggie was still at my side and the coolness of the water, as it trickled down my throat, momentarily consoled me. Gazing at the forbidden drawer, I imagined a combination lock gripped around the handle attached to a large metal chain—only I didn't know the code to unlock it. I was being denied access; that's a good thing, I thought. I put the glass in the sink carefully and left the kitchen. I decided to get dressed and go to the courts. I'd be safe there, I thought. I wouldn't be alone—somebody would take care of me.

As I backed out of the driveway, my sweaty palms grasped the steering wheel tightly in fear of losing control. The dashboard appeared closer than I remembered, and the needle on the speedometer glowed at the 30 miles per hour mark, then at 35 miles per hour as I made my way toward the safe haven of the tennis courts. I paid close attention to tracking the yellow line as it clearly designated the curves in the road and distinguished the lane I was driving in from the oncoming traffic. It was as if I were following the yellow brick road; maybe I would meet up with the Cowardly Lion or the Tin Man or Scarecrow, I thought. I felt like I was Dorothy seeking out the Wizard of Oz to help me find my own Auntie Em. It put a smile on my face for a moment. My rescuer was "Somewhere Over the Rainbow." Suddenly bright red taillights came upon me from the left. My car skidded and swerved to the right, as I slammed on my brakes to avoid rear-ending the guy in front of me as he stopped for a light. Without warning, anxiety took over my entire being. Dorothy was gone as quickly as she came. Time to get back to reality, I thought. Still, I realized that God must be watching me, and I arrived at my destination unscathed.

I will always remember the look on my friend Nicky's face when she greeted me on the steps at the entrance to the courts. Her furrowed brow and the look in her eyes mirrored my pain, making me even more frightened.

"What are you doing here? You look like Hell. You're coming with me to my house right now. I am going to get you help," she said, grabbing my arm and ushering me to her car.

We sat in her living room as I listened to her phone conversation with her psychologist.

"My friend is having a breakdown and I am afraid she will hurt herself."

She confirmed my appointment for that afternoon. When I left, she hugged me and presented me with a book. "Read this, it will help you understand what's happening to you," she said.

The book was entitled, *Peace From Nervous Suffering*, by Claire Weekes.

I realized that if my life were a dance card, I had gone from the romance of the Foxtrot during my early courtship and marriage to Arty to the crazed, frenetic Lindy Hop of my experimental phase to a far more depressing dance, the dance of the Blues. What was in store for me next, I wondered.

- ♪ ♪ ♪ -

The Twist

The Twist is performed with feet shoulder width apart.
The torso is kept squared to the knees and hips, and
the torso and legs rotate on the balls of the feet.
The feet grind back and forth on the floor.
The partners who dance together both gyrate
but they never touch.

The Shrink

**I couldn't even leave my house before
therapy, but there was a new "twist"
in the dance of life ahead.**

I paced the floor of the waiting room, clutching the book Nicky
had given to me. Looking around at the caramel painted walls
lined with bookcases, I tried to relax. My pacing slowed as I heard
the musak playing softly in the background. Feeling calmer, I sat on
a beige velour club chair and glanced at the books on the shelves. My
inner chaos quieted and I felt safe until I noticed the book, entitled
On Death and Dying, right in front of me. Once again, my heart
began to race. My fingertips felt raw to the touch as if I had put them
through a grater and taken off a layer of skin. What was happening
to me? Was I going to die?

Suddenly the door to an office opened and Mr. Hirsch, a tall,
slender, well dressed man with light brown wavy hair, introduced
himself.

"Hi, I'm Mr. Hirsch. Come in, Mrs. Levy, and take a seat," he said, pointing to the black leather chair in the corner. His deep blue eyes and distinguished features reminded me of a clean shaven apostle. Looking at him, I imagined a halo around his head—he must be related to God. He would be my savior.

I sat on the edge of the chair. My body was stiff; the soles of my shoes seemed glued to the short napped, wheat-colored carpet. I felt like a china doll that would shatter into pieces if I were to fall.

Mr. Hirsch was soft spoken and had a sincere smile. He asked me to provide him with some background on my life and my situation. Not sure of what to expect, I spoke slowly at first choosing my words carefully, but after a while, I began to express my feelings without inhibition. I needed someone to listen, someone to understand, someone with compassion, someone who could help make me better. My words came out quickly, as I told Mr. Hirsch about my anxiety attacks leading up to my incident in the pool. He took pages of notes, on a legal sized yellow pad. I remember asking him if he thought that I was suicidal. At the end of my fifty-five minute session, he assured me that I would not take my life or harm myself.

"I'd like to see you twice a week. I will review my data and during your next visit, you will have my diagnosis," he said. Shaking his hand as I left, his voice rang in my ears—you're not suicidal, you're not going to kill yourself. His words were the gospel. I trusted and believed in him. After all, he was my new savior.

"How are you feeling, Mrs. Levy?" Mr. Hirsh asked, two days later. "Have you had any more incidents?"

I felt better, but still vulnerable. I was glad to be sitting with

Mr. Hirsch again.

"I have completed my diagnosis. You have agoraphobia. It is treatable as long as you are willing to do the work on yourself," Mr. Hirsch told me as he referred to his notes. "Agoraphobia is a phobia and can be a severe anxiety condition stemming from a crisis. It could have been the anaphylactic shock that triggered your breakdown. Regardless of where it stems from, agoraphobics feel safe at home, and as in your case, they refrain from being in situations in which they feel threatened."

"What do I have to do to get better? Is there medication I can take? What is the process and how long will it take?" I enquired nervously.

"You have to stand on your own two legs, not your husband's, not your mother's, not your friend's," he said pointing to my pants. I tightened my quad muscles and squeezed them until they bulged against my denim jeans. "Trust your own judgments and decisions. Take Valium only in an emergency."

Easier said than done, I thought as I left his office.

That evening I lay in bed and reached for the book, *Peace from Nervous Suffering*, which Nicky had given to me. As I flipped through the pages, the word agoraphobic popped out at me. I didn't want to read about this mental illness. It scared me. So I closed the book and placed it in my night table drawer as if I were locking it up. A month later, I finally mustered up the courage to read it. The book became my newest security blanket.

- ♪ ♩ ♪ -

"I'm fucking scared," I said to Mr. Hirsch, as I leaned over staring at my feet. This was our third session.

"What's frightening you?"

"If I knew that then I wouldn't be sitting here," I said defensively, as my body squirmed helplessly. Hesitating, I cleared my throat and suddenly the words flowed effortlessly. "I want to tell you something. It's about my father."

"Don't be afraid, your father is not here. He can't hear you."

There was silence as I looked around the room checking every corner to be sure. I took a deep breath.

"I'm not sure if I love my father." I took another deep breath. "In fact, I know that I don't love my father." My voice went up a pitch. "Does that make me a bad person? The Ten Commandments tell you to honor thy mother and father, but how can I honor him if I don't love him?"

I tried to hold back my tears as Mr. Hirsch handed me a tissue. Placing my hands across my face, I began to sob. Trying to catch my breath, I made gasping sounds. After a few moments my sobbing subsided. I blew my nose and wiped my swollen red eyes. "Am I a bad person?" I asked, looking for reassurance.

He shook his head, "It's healthy to acknowledge your feelings," he told me.

"Your father abused you emotionally. Emotional abuse strips away self esteem and leaves hidden scars that can manifest in insecurity especially when it comes from a figure in authority. Understanding these feelings makes it easier to accept them."

I left the session feeling relieved. I wasn't a bad person for not loving my father. I had been validated by Mr. Hirsch, an important figure of authority in my life.

Looking in my bathroom mirror, I smiled. I like myself, I'm good, I'm pretty, I'm smart, I affirmed. My smile got bigger as these positive thoughts filled my head. I rubbed my fingertips together to confirm that I was getting better. They weren't raw anymore—I put them to my lips and kissed them. "I'm taking care of me, I'm taking care of me," I said aloud and reached into my makeup case for the brightest lipstick I could find.

- ♪ ♪ ♪ -

I kept seeing Mr. Hirsch twice a week, and slowly I began to feel better. We continued talking about my father and soon after I started to also share my feelings about my mother. I told Mr. Hirsch that I loved my mother, but my sensitivity to criticism wouldn't allow me to speak with her. "She does guilt," I said as I rubbed my palms together. "She continually asks me to take her to visit her father at the senior living center in Long Beach, and when I refuse she scolds me as if I were still her little girl. I can't take her nagging voice telling me I am doing something wrong." Almost apologizing, I looked Mr. Hirsch directly in his eyes and said, "You know how mothers can be? I know she means well, but I can't deal with her now."

I didn't realize my phobia still lingered until Arty took me to Vermont for a weekend in early August. Upon reaching Southern Vermont, my eyes widened as I observed the towering Green Mountains. The steepness of these high masses overwhelmed me. Their peaks disappeared into the clouds reminding me of stories I had read in childhood of giants who had immense power.

"Arty, look at the size of the mountains, they're closing in on me, I can't escape them," I said as I crouched in the seat of the car. "I want to go home. I want to go home now."

"It's your imagination. You know these mountains; we've skied them; we've hiked them;" Arty said. "They're mountains, not monsters. Take a deep breath; we'll be at the motel in a few minutes."

I couldn't let go of my fear. We returned home that evening.

After the trip I seemed to regress. Most of all I feared criticism from my friends, especially Annie, the one who had introduced me to pot. She constantly badgered me about my weight, which caused me anxiety and made me hang up on her. Our once daily phone conversations became non-existent. I asked Mr. Hirsch about this during one of our sessions.

"Your anxiety disorder relates to your fear. You don't want to hear Annie tell you that you're gaining weight. That signals that you are bad and those thoughts can trigger a panic attack." Mr. Hirsch said. "Hearing her say you're getting fat can be degrading and embarrass you. You'll know when you're ready to speak with Annie. See you next week."

I left thinking about what the doctor had said. What am I afraid of? What am I trying to control? I walked home and thought about calling Annie that night.

- ♪ ♪ ♪ -

"We were invited to sail with friends to Nantucket, and you

think that I should go, despite my anxiety attacks? Well, I don't. I don't feel comfortable. I'm afraid. I'm safe at home," I told Mr. Hirsch at our next session.

I was happy I was sitting back in the black leather chair sharing my thoughts with Mr. Hirsch. I must be making progress, I thought.

"I can't go on this trip. I'll be away too long and the boat isn't air conditioned. I could have night sweats or shortness of breath; what would I do then?" I asked. "What if its buggy or I have an allergic reaction to fish?"

"Nantucket is a beautiful island," Mr. Hirsch said, reaching for a photo album to show me some pictures. "I've been there. It's beautiful. There are lots of shops and the streets are quaint." He pointed to a picture of the Brant Point Lighthouse at the entrance of the Harbor.

I smiled as I glanced through his pictures.

"It's important for you to try this. If you think that the sailing trip is too long then plan something shorter or go out to dinner once a week. Make dates with friends who are less threatening. Every new outing will build your confidence."

"OK, OK, I'll give it some thought," I said as I shook his hand and left.

Arty called his friend the next day and made plans for us to go. "But just for a week," I hollered.

- ♪ ♪ ♪ -

I continued working at the travel agency part time, but most of my hours were spent at the tennis courts. My little black book filled with tennis games made me feel accepted. Still haunted by my childhood loneliness, I looked to these women to be my friends only to learn their primary interest was in having a good tennis game. I never heard from them off the courts. Wanting to understand my tennis relationships, I focused numerous therapy sessions around them and learned to be discriminating about which women I'd befriend.

I remember having lunch at the club with a woman who was mourning her mother's death.

She cried as she told me of her terrible loss and shared with me that she had difficulty getting through each day. She couldn't believe her mother was gone and waited every morning at her front door for her mother to return. I told her I had been seeing a therapist for six weeks to deal with my own parental issues, and I suggested she make an appointment with him.

"I couldn't leave my house before I went into therapy," I told her. "Now, I am able to dine out with friends, and I enjoy tennis more than ever. Prior to seeing Mr. Hirsch, I'd follow the tennis ladies as if I were a puppy dog with my tail between my legs, panting for recognition. He helped me so much, that I know Mr. Hirsch can help you, too."

She made an appointment, but her visits were short lived.

When I saw her back at the courts she told me that she had stopped seeing him because he wasn't able to help her.

Feeling strong enough to question Mr. Hirsch, I asked out of curiosity, "Why did she stop seeing you? She was a mess and could barely function. You've done such wonders for me why couldn't you do the same for her?"

"In order to heal from any mental distress, whether its depression or phobias, it's up to the individual who is suffering to change," Mr. Hirsch told me. "We can only control our own actions, not the actions of others," he continued. "Your friend expected everyone around her to change. You, on the other hand, are getting better because you've made the change; you went through the process to achieve a healthy goal," he said. "Remember when we started I told you not depend on others and to stand on your own two legs? You've done it. You're now an independent woman." I stood up, gave him a hug and ran out of his office as if I just won a race.

Arty was supportive throughout most of my agoraphobic crisis, but there were moments when he lost patience. I remember one day telling him that I wanted to go for a manicure, but feared being in the nail salon. "Everyone will look at me as if I am crazy," I told him. He looked at me with disdain, shook his fist, and said, "What can happen to you? You're only having your nails done."

Why was he yelling?, I wondered. I remember standing on my screened in porch looking out at the pool. Arty sat on the blue and white floral couch, reading. I was confused by his lack of patience since I knew that he wanted me to be healthy. I sat next to him. "Arty, please understand what I am going through. I want to be better, but I just can't help myself."

Arty put his book in his lap and said, "I do understand, but it's enough already. You are making great progress, and I think if you don't go to have your nails done, you'll set yourself back. Ro, go get your nails done," he continued. "You will feel like a new person when you come home." Almost pleading he said, "If you can't do it for yourself, do it for me."

His guilt forced me to make the decision. I went to the salon and had them paint my nails bright orange.

- ♪ ♪ ♪ -

I don't exactly remember why, but making the decision to go to the nail salon was a turning point in me getting well. Rather than relying on Arty's courage or guilt to spur me into action, I began taking charge of my life. I went back to speaking to my mother and Annie on a regular basis. I became able to set boundaries with other people; finally I was confident enough to shrug off people's derogatory remarks or firmly tell them to stop putting me down. The trip to Nantucket was better than I could have imagined. As I confronted each situation I deemed threatening, my fears began to dissolve.

As I think back to this difficult period, I realize there were four factors that helped me get well: Arty's support, Mr. Hirsch's guidance, my wanting to change, and the love from my kids. I'm not sure, however, if my kids ever realized what I went through. I didn't try to hide my panic attacks from them, but their presence was a soothing force. I don't remember ever feeling anxious when they were around. Arty stood by me and tried not to react to my crazy behavior. At my core, I believe his survival instinct was truly what saved us.

As the summer was coming to an end, I knew I was healing. I no longer relied on Arty or anyone else to make my decisions for me, and I had replaced my fear with the confidence that I had the judgment and resources I needed to function in the outside world. I planned weekly dinner dates with friends and enjoyed controversial conversations without feeling personally attacked.

"Arty, let's go back to the Green Mountains in Vermont next weekend," I said one day as I looked out the window, noticing the leaves begin to change colors. "I'll ask the nanny to stay with the kids. It will be like a mini honeymoon."

"Great idea," he responded.

It had been two months since our first trip to the mountains, and this time instead of feeling overpowered, I was *empowered*. The brisk air invigorated me as I hiked 3284 feet to the summit of Bromley Mountain. Arty and I enjoyed a picnic lunch as we sat on a wooden lookout and gazed at the beauty of the horizon and valley below. Looking up at the clear blue sky, I started to sing the song, "I'm Sitting On Top of The World," as if the heavens could hear me. Smiling at me, Arty hummed along. Before we started our trek back down, we carved our initials and the date in one of the posts. "We'll be back," I said as I grabbed Arty's hand.

It was mid October, 1978. I had been seeing Mr. Hirsch since the second week in July. After I got back from my vacation, I walked into his office feeling as if I owned a piece of it and took my customary seat in the corner.

"You've made great strides in a very short time," he told me. "Your negative thoughts have turned to positive ones; you have become assertive and self-assured. You are an independent, free thinking woman and as a result of your tremendous improvement, I am cutting down your visits to once a week." His genuine smile, baring his perfect white teeth authenticated his words.

"Are you sure? Can I survive seeing you only once a week?" Stunned by his words, I felt tightness in my upper body. Trying to rid myself of the discomfort, I sat straight up pinching my shoulder blades together.

"I know you can handle it. If I thought differently I wouldn't be changing our schedule," he said. "If you feel the need to talk, call me. In the meantime, I'll see you next Tuesday."

Closing his office door behind me, I thought, next Tuesday is such a long way off. How will I get through the week? Intellectually I understood his decision, but emotionally I rattled with uncertainty.

Much to my surprise, the week went by without any glitches. Since the outdoor tennis club was closing for the winter, I joined an indoor league to keep my competitive juices flowing and fill up some of my idle time. Working two, sometimes three, days at the travel agency kept me occupied too. With Mitchell and Gary in high school, Kenny almost ten and Tracy about to turn eight, my kids were independent and less needy of my attention.

I needed new challenges to stimulate my transformation. What new "Twist" in the dance of my life lay ahead of me, and would I be flexible enough to handle it?

- ♪ ♪ ♪ -

Junkanoo

The dance called Junkanoo is an energetic,
colorful parade of brightly costumed people
gyrating and dancing
to the rhythmic accompaniment
of cowbells, drums and whistles.
It is most often performed
at Bahamian Festivals.

The Minister Has To Sign It

Unbeknownst to me the Festival of Junkanoo
would help me celebrate and
free me from my past.

*I*n mid November, 1978, a friend of mine, who I had worked part-time with for many years in a retail travel agency and who now represented a boutique hotel in the Caribbean, phoned to tell me about a job opening. I had been searching for a new challenge. My voice went up an octave, and without taking a breath I impulsively asked, "WHO, WHEN, WHERE, WHAT, what do I have to do?"

"It's a sales position and I think you're perfect for the job," she said. "You have great people skills, and the job entails building relationships with travel agents. Contact Manny Rich, Sales Manager at Caribbean Holidays; he's expecting your call."

The possibility of having a sales position in a big tour company was a great opportunity for me. I realized that this was my chance to finally start building a career. By traveling to New York City every day by train, and working full time, I just knew that I'd discover a whole new world. I'd be like Christopher Columbus, and the train would be either my Nina, Pinta, or Santa Maria. I was filled with delight at the possibilities.

My interview was set for the first week in December. My spirits were high. It was hard to believe that only a few months ago, I had been emotionally paralyzed, barely able to function or leave my house. I sensed my mind and body were finally friends, and I was filled with relief.

I worried about what to wear to the interview. With only two weeks left to find the perfect business outfit, I obsessively spent every day shopping at boutiques and department stores trying on everything from multi-colored dresses to conservative navy or black suits. I even tried on a tight fitting grey knit short skirt, which made me feel sexy. Ultimately, I bought a blue and white flared knee length skirt with tan trim and a matching top with three quarter length puffy sleeves. It was simple, yet professional.

The big day finally arrived. I dressed and checked my reflection in the mirror to make sure every hair was in place. As I slicked on my lipstick, I smacked my lips together as if I were sealing a well wrapped present. I was a gift, I thought, and Caribbean Holidays would be the ideal recipient.

"Good morning, I have an appointment with Manny Rich," I said to the receptionist as I gazed around the office. Framed travel posters depicting Caribbean destinations hung on the walls. The posters reflected the beauty of these islands and whet my appetite with a desire to travel.

"Ms. Levy, I'm Steve Press, Manny Rich's counterpart and I will escort you to our office," a man with dark brown eyes and salt and pepper hair said with a smile.

I shook his hand and said, "Nice to meet you."

Steve walked me through the office pointing out three large circular reservation desks. "This is the hub of the office; the sales department is in the back," Steve said.

Enthusiasm built as I entered the sales office. Manny, a tall lanky man in his mid thirties with dark wavy hair sat behind an antique oak desk butted up against Steve's desk which was identical. Greeting me with a warm smile, he said, "You come highly recommended."

Both men were extremely friendly and asked me targeted questions about my strengths and weaknesses. I told them that my greatest strength was my adaptability, relaying a story about how I handled one of my difficult travel clients who called me from the airport screaming, "It's raining, and the weather report didn't call for rain. Why didn't you tell me to fly out tomorrow? This trip is costing me a fortune and now it's raining!"

I explained to them how I quieted my client's anxiety by telling him it was just a brief shower.

"Put your mind in vacation mode," I told my client. "Go to the bar, order a rum punch, and take a sip. Close your eyes, and visualize lying on a chaise on the beach with the sun baking your body. Oh, and please send me a postcard with the weather report." I told Steve and Manny that my client instantly calmed down. I looked at them with a big smile and said, "I should have been a shrink, or better yet a weatherman!"

Laughing, Manny said with authority, "You're hired."

I started my new job as sales manager the first week of January, 1979.

- ♪ ♪ ♪ -

My first day of work, I arrived promptly at 9:00 a.m. Steve took me to my office and Manny introduced me to my trainer, telling me it would take about two weeks to fully understand my position. My trainer was thorough as he explained that some agencies refused to use us because we didn't pay additional commissions or overrides to the agents. He explained to me that we were competing with other tour companies who based their sales on volume and set annual quotas for agents, thus locking them in around the money. The way it worked was the more trips the agents sold and booked, the bigger the commission the agents made. This was a real challenge, he explained, but the conversion was possible. "Sell yourself to them first, and once you've gained their trust, you will win them over," he said.

I took time to familiarize myself with our tour packages and to understand the process of booking a trip as well as to get to know the reservation agents personally. Believing that the company I was working for had impeccable credentials, I was confident from the start, but whether it was a conscious or a subconscious choice, I made a deliberate decision to only call upon our preferred agents where I was sure I wouldn't be rejected.

- ♪ ♪ ♪ -

"We don't use Caribbean Holidays because they don't pay overrides to our agents." Marge said, barely acknowledging my presence as I walked through the door. She was the owner of the first non-preferred agency I called on, the beginning of my second week on the road. Marge, a woman in her mid thirties with bleached blonde hair, bordered on obesity and had a slovenly appearance (later on, when I got to know her, her jovial personality changed my initial negative impression of her). I watched that day as she shuffled a pile of papers on her desk. The phone hung in the crook of her neck close to her ear freeing up her hands so that she could sign travel documents while continuing to stuff her face with junk food. Not wanting to judge, I decided to concentrate on converting her as I took a seat at her desk.

"Would you like a Twinkie?" she asked unwrapping the cellophane with one of her free hands.

"No thanks, I just had lunch."

How interesting that the ice was broken around food, I thought, as we began to discuss business. Her obsession with food softened her up. I must remember this, I thought, and bring her a box lunch next time.

"I understand your reasons for not using Caribbean Holidays," I said, using a soft sell tactic. "But I'd like to suggest that you give us a try for your discerning clientele; the ones that require more handholding and more attention; the ones who are seeking the perfect vacation. As I am sure you are aware, we are a customer service oriented company and are known as the Rolls Royce of the travel industry. We have the utmost respect from the airlines and hotels, and this mutual respect results in our obtaining large blocks of rooms and seats during peak and holiday seasons. If you use us sporadically for your high-end clients, it will give you the opportunity to experience the difference without forfeiting any substantial commissions, while at the time you'll also be assured that your special clientele will be 100% satisfied."

Sitting back in my chair, I took a deep breath. I felt as if I was on a soapbox, yet I knew I was convincing. I looked at Marge and smiled as I watched her stuff her mouth with the last bite of her Twinkie. Her wide-eyed expression told me she was interested. The sugar from the Twinkie must have kicked in, I figured.

"OK, OK, I'll give you a try as long as it won't affect my bottom line and my top clients are satisfied, but the first time I have a problem, you're out, understood?"

Nodding in agreement, I told her she would not regret the decision to work with us.

I left feeling as if I had run a marathon.

During dinner that evening I told Arty of my day's activities, and after describing Marge and her food addictions to him, Arty dubbed her "Large Marge" without ever having met her. Perhaps he was judging, but it made me laugh so hard I almost fell off my chair. He was so funny and I loved him for his humor. From that day on I always thought of her as "Large Marge," but the secret of her nickname was safely held between me and Arty.

- ♪ ♪ ♪ -

Working at Caribbean Holidays was an invaluable experience. It played a positive role in my emotional healing. I learned I was capable of anything I set my mind to. I made new friends and relished their respect and acceptance. I was a saleswoman, a successful one and deep inside, I finally started to believe it.

And there were other perks to the job. Familiarization trips (fam trips), during which I was "wined and dined" at the best hotels and restaurants for a nominal cost, gave me the opportunity to visit exotic destinations I'd only heard of. I remember my trip to Panama, San Blas Island, and the Panama Canal. Standing at the Canal waving to people on large cruise ships was thrilling; I was so close that I could have shaken hands with the passengers as they passed through the locks. It was like being a part of history, connecting the East and the West. I wished Arty could have been with me to share that moment.

Prior to this, tennis had been my life, limiting me to those whose interests revolved around nothing else but the competitive game. I was pleased with the direction my life was now taking. I was hungry for and welcomed every new experience that increased my knowledge and skills.

"Are you coming to the LIARS lunch today?" Linda, one of my travel colleagues, asked me one day.

"Are you insinuating I'm a liar? What do you mean, is it a lunch for liars?" I asked her, laughing.

"It's the Long Island Area Reps; for short we call ourselves the LIARS," she told me with amusement in her voice. "As a Sales Rep for Long Island, you qualify and you're welcome to participate."

In addition to taking us away from the daily grind of calling on agents, these luncheons were highly educational. Each month, a sales rep from a different travel entity would be the host. He or she would choose the restaurant, send out the invitations, distribute the promotional materials, and give a brief presentation about his or her product or destination. I particularly enjoyed the lunches hosted by international airline reps as it allowed me to vicariously travel to foreign destinations as I viewed their presentations.

But as I got to know the people, I realized these luncheons were an escape for many of them. Johnny, always with a drink in his hand, was tall, his golden blonde hair, distinct features, and green eyes reminded me of a Greek god—all he needed was a white toga draped around his torso. As our friendship developed, he told me he was unhappy with his job and his personal life. I felt as if he were looking to me for answers. Jim, also guzzling down his alcohol, was always flirting with the women, slapping their asses or resting his arm on their shoulders. He was balding, in his late forties with a vibrant personality, and made it clear to anyone who would listen that he couldn't wait for retirement. Amy, an attractive woman with long black hair and dark brown eyes, who concealed the dark rings under her eyes with cover-up, was unhappily married. She told me that her husband had no ambition. Perhaps she should hook up with Johnny or Jim, I thought. Observing the cross section of people made it obvious many were running from their daily routines by heavily drinking. My demeanor must have reflected my stability as many of these colleagues now looked to me as their sounding board. The fact that I had risen from a place of darkness enabled me to be compassionate, listen to their mental distress, and offer sound advice. Even though I was not professionally trained, instinctively I related; understanding their needs I responded accordingly. I had become a "pseudo shrink."

- ♪ ♪ ♪ -

After working at Caribbean Holidays a little less than two years, Manny summoned me into his office. Meeting with him every Monday to discuss my week's sales calls, I was used to seeing him behind his oversized, antique oak desk, only this day sitting up particularly straight he appeared to tower over the desk. I realized something was going on. Taking a seat, I nervously twiddled my thumbs as I waited to hear what he had to say. Clearing his throat, he dropped the bomb.

"We have to let you go. Our sales are declining and we're losing business to the overrides. The CEO cannot justify your continued employment. However," he said his voice lightening up a bit, "the good news is, I spoke with a friend at the Bahamas Tourist Office who is aware of your accomplishments and wants to meet with you to discuss a position."

Although I was shocked, I maintained my composure and didn't fall back into a catatonic state or doubt my abilities, but truthfully, I was sad to leave the company. Despite his firing of me, I admired Manny; moreover, his recommendation acknowledged my achievements and endorsed my qualifications. I thanked him for the referral, refusing to allow my dismissal to take me down. As I left the office for the last time, I thought, it's their loss.

The company went out of business shortly thereafter, and I like to believe that terminating me was an important contributing factor to their demise.

- ♪ ♪ ♪ -

Kenny and Tracy, my two youngest children, and I danced around my bedroom holding hands and singing, "The Minister has to sign it! The Minister has to sign it!" I felt confident and excited about my forthcoming job at the Bahamas Tourist Office.

The New York District Manager had told me, "you're hired but we must follow protocol and wait for the Minister of the Bahamas to sign the document, authorizing your appointment."

Awaiting the Minister's signature, my old friend, anxiety, appeared once again. Although I was confident the Minister would sign the document, until there was confirmation, I couldn't rest. His signature would be my seal of approval, confirming I was qualified to do the job; more importantly, it confirmed my recognition as a valued individual. With all this at stake, it was virtually impossible to remain calm.

Two days later, I got the phone call.

"He signed it," the District Manager said. Jumping up and down with joy, I started to loudly sing, "The Minister signed it, the Minister signed it." Kenny and Tracy ran to the kitchen and joined me in the song. I hugged my kids, feeling ecstatic, like a little girl who had just received a gift. I tried to visualize what the Minister looked like, but the Wizard of Oz came to mind, sitting on his throne in Emerald City behind an extra-large desk wearing a top hat and dressed in a black tuxedo. In my mind's eye, holding a small block with the Bahamian logo, he raised his hand and pressed the stamp firmly to the contract, officially approving my appointment.

I started my new position at the Bahamas Tourist Office

(BTO) the first week of January 1981. As in my last position, my job description included calling on travel agents and promoting tourism to the Bahamas and their family of smaller islands known as their "Out Islands." I was a Regional Sales Manager for the Northeast and my territory included the tri-state area, sometimes taking me into New England. After two weeks of training and a visit to the Bahamas to familiarize myself, I returned home excited to sell this destination—the hotels were beautiful and appealed to all budgets, and the beaches were some of the most impressive I had ever seen. This would be an easy sell, so I thought.

To my dismay, I quickly learned that this third world country was not a desired vacation spot. The Bahamas had a bad reputation: American tourists claimed the Bahamian people emanated an attitude of arrogance and indifference and made them feel unwelcome. The tourists claimed that the Bahamians ignored the guests in the restaurants and neglected serving them at the pool and the beach. This, combined with a daily temperature that often didn't rise higher than 70 degrees during the winter season, proved to be a deterrent to new visitors.

On the other hand, the Bahamas was a progressive independent nation and the government was determined to overcome their bad reputation. Therefore, the administration in power, wanting to be sure tourism would come back, implemented a mandatory training program for all employees who worked in the hotels and other tourist related jobs. Expert hoteliers were brought in to educate the Bahamians on the importance of good service.

"Park your disinterest and aloofness at the door," said one of the hoteliers teaching a class on how to treat guests when visiting their country.

- ♪ ♪ ♪ -

The word Bahamas is derived from the Spanish words "baja mar" which means shallow sea and is an archipelago of over 700 islands with the clearest waters in the world. The trade winds make the climate perfect year round; 70 to 75 in the winter, spring, and fall; 80 to 85 in summer. The laid back attitude of the Bahamians is sometimes misunderstood, but actually, "they are a humorous, fun loving people," a marketing person who developed the "It's Better in the Bahamas" ad campaign told me. He said I should push the night life, the casinos, and the varieties of the islands.

One of my big ideas was to bring the Bahamas to the public. I thought about Junkanoo, the National Festival in the Bahamas, which is completely unique to the area. The name "Junkanoo" is said to come from the name "John Canoe," an African tribal chief who demanded the right to celebrate with his people after being brought as slaves to the West Indies. This evocative celebration is similar to the Mardi Gras in New Orleans and Carnival in Rio. The rhythms of drums, whistles, cowbells, and washboards create an infectious beat causing people to gyrate as they parade down the street. That's it, I thought. I'll create mock Junkanoo Festivals; I can do this in malls and co-partner with travel agents, it will be a win-win for everyone. Having just returned from experiencing this festival first hand, I knew if I exposed prospective vacationers to the energetic colorful parade of brightly costumed people dancing, they'd be sure to remember the Bahamas and make it their number one vacation spot. Drafting my preliminary plan at my desk, the music of the Junkanoo resonated in my brain, and I spun my chair around. My feet barely touched the floor as my elation heightened.

I planned my first mock Junkanoo parade promotion with a couple who owned a travel agency in Long Island. I was particularly fond of this husband and wife team—both with disabilities requiring the use of wheelchairs—they had overcome many obstacles and persevered at building a successful travel business. Susan, a petite woman with short black hair, was perky and never allowed her disability to get in the way. She maneuvered her wheelchair with ease as she pushed the joystick on her armrest to the right or left, enabling her to greet clients as they walked through the door. Mark, a man with a large frame, appeared muscular, perhaps as a result of physical therapy. He handled his chair as if he were driving a car. Just like a kid, he'd speed around the agency making sharp turns, and attempting "wheelies" which attracted attention. Good service was his priority and he made it his business to see that each customer was being taken care of. Since I had a lot of respect for them, I thought that a mock Junkanoo parade promotion would be a good opportunity to help them attract more customers.

After hearing my plan, Susan looked at Mark and said excitedly, "Let's set the date now. It's the middle of winter, what better time to promote a vacation in the Bahamas?"

We worked together to create recipes and menus for specialty Bahamian foods: conch (pronounced konk) chowder, conch fritters, conch salad, and typical Bahamian rum drinks, such as Bahama Mamas and the Goombay Smash. We decided that we would offer a tasting of these mouth-watering foods and samples of the delicious sweet rum drinks distributed during the festivities. I organized a group of people from my office to stage the Junkanoo and designed colorful costumes from crepe paper that were carefully glued to fabric or cardboard and worn by every participant as they marched around the mall. Painted faces or masks added to the brilliance of the elaborate colors.

Finally, the day we had been waiting for arrived. It was mid February, and the temperature hovered just above 32 degrees with a fresh snowfall on the ground. People filed into the mall to get away from the cold and were swept away by the rhythmic sounds of our Junkanoo, which included whistles, cow bells, and Goombay drums made from goatskin. I set up a table in front of the agency and arranged for Mark and Susan to sit on each side of me. A large banner reading "It's Better In the Bahamas" was tied across two poles above the table. We displayed Bahamian products in a mini "Straw Market," which included large conch shells that people could put to their ear and hear the sounds of the ocean. Small plates with delicacies and cups with refreshing rum drinks were available for people to sample.

The recurring beat of the music drew hordes of people to our table. We were so busy we could hardly keep up with the questions as people surrounded our table waiting to taste the samples of conch and the sugary rum punch. Licking their lips, they devoured the food and drink while they inquired about gambling, beaches, rates for honeymoons, families, and singles, and took home promotional brochures featuring highlights of the Bahamas and their family of Out Islands. The attendees particularly liked the proximity of these islands to the United States and the fact that the Bahamas was an affordable vacation, a perfect get-away for a long weekend. The general consensus was that the Bahamas were easy to get to, inexpensive, and offered something for everyone. We were gratified to hear these positive comments over and over throughout the day.

As I thought back over the past two months, the combination of navigating my relationships with the Bahamians and the agents, the trade shows, sales blitzes, cocktail receptions, and mock Junkanoo promotions reaffirmed I was an instrumental part in helping to change the image of the Bahamas.

I left the office for the day and headed downtown to catch my train feeling empowered and proud of my accomplishments.

- ♪ ♪ ♪ -

February 27, 1981

It was a beautiful day, 60 degrees, not a cloud in the sky; hard to believe it was still winter. Dressing for the weather, I wore aqua blue linen pants, and a short-sleeved white silk blouse with blue and red flowers characteristic of the tropics. I smiled broadly as I opened my front door, picturing myself in a Bahamian photo op. All I needed was a Bahama Mama in one hand, conch fritters in the other, with a straw bag hanging from my shoulder to complete my look.

Reviewing my sales log, I decided to travel to the northern suburbs to enjoy the spring-like weather. It was a good choice as budding trees were easily visible, and I did not hear any complaints about unfriendly Bahamians or the cool weather. On the contrary, most agents told me that this was the biggest selling January and

February for the Bahamas they had had in years. "It must be better in the Bahamas," an agent called out as I left my last sales call and headed home. The day was perfect and I was in good spirits.

It was 6:00 p.m. Arty and I worked side-by-side preparing dinner—he was marinating chicken for the grill and I was cutting vegetables for the salad. The phone rang.

"You get it," I said, as I opened the fridge looking for more greens.

"What happened?" I heard him say to the person on the other end of the phone line.

His expression immediately told me something was wrong. I stopped chopping cucumbers and went to him reaching out for the phone. Shaking his head in disbelief, he quietly said, "Your mother is dead."

I didn't grasp what he was saying. My mother was on vacation in Ocho Rios, Jamaica with a friend and was coming home today. This couldn't be true, people didn't die on vacation—people go on vacation to relax and have fun. Grabbing the phone from him, I heard a woman's voice telling me my mother had not felt well prior to boarding the plane; her color was pale white and they had to put her in a wheelchair. I couldn't believe what I was hearing.

"Where is her friend?" I asked.

Afraid I was going to fall, Arty brought me over to a chair and sat me down as I gripped the phone tighter. The woman, a nurse, told me my mother boarded the plane, and shortly after it took off, the pilot turned turn back to Montego Bay as my mother suffered a heart attack. I was in shock.

"I want to speak to her friend, I want to hear what happened.

This can't be true, put her on the phone," I screamed.

Her travel partner was a dear old friend. I knew she would tell me the truth, and at that moment in time, she was the only connection I had to my mother. I wanted to hear that my mother was not dead. Overwhelmed by grief, my heart ached.

"Did she have a good time, did she have a good time?" I repeated over and over. My mother's friend's words were all a blur, I couldn't concentrate, I couldn't think. I began to cry as Arty held me tightly in his arms.

Slumping in the chair, I hung up the phone. Arty and I just stared at each other in disbelief.

We had to tell the kids. They loved their grandma so much. The kids always got excited when she brought them little yellow butterscotch candies and gifts wrapped in crumpled tissue paper. She taught Ken and Tracy how to play casino and enjoyed competitive gin rummy games with Mitchell and Gary. Thinking of their close relationship with her, my sorrow intensified.

Mitchell and Gary were at college, and Kenny was hanging out with a friend. Tracy was the only one at home when we received the call. Arty called out for her as I was unable to see, hear, or sense what was going on. Upon hearing the shocking news, she hugged me. It must have been confusing, as she was only eleven.

During the ride to my father's house, I recalled that I had introduced my mother to the world of travel when she was sixty years old. Once she started there was no stopping her. I remembered the last time I had seen her. In preparation for her vacation, I had brought her a portable luggage carrier that she could use to wheel her suitcase around in, so she wouldn't be burdened by pushing around a heavy weight. Before she left on the trip, I noticed she was pale. She said she had not been feeling well.

"I need to get away; your father doesn't want to go, so I decided to travel with my good friend. I know the vacation will do me good," she said. I made her promise she would go to the doctor if she still didn't feel well when she returned. As I pulled out from her driveway, I had watched her reflection in the rear view mirror. She was wearing a blue flowered housedress with a stained apron tied around her waist. Holding a dishtowel in her left hand, she waved goodbye as she watched me drive away. This was a ritual with her, as if she was making sure I was OK. I will hold this final vision of her forever in my heart.

As Arty drove, I thought it was ironic that I was on my way to tell my father about my mother's death. I knew her friend wouldn't call him as she had no relationship with him but had a special fondness for me. My head ached, my heart was heavy, and suddenly the realization hit me. I had feared my father my whole life, and now I would be destined to care for him for the rest of his years—and ultimately I did. Perhaps it was fate, as I cared for my father for twelve years after my mother's death. It was during those years I really got to know and understand him. My parting words upon his death were, "Dad, I love you."

Amidst a blanket of grief and fear, I wondered if I would ever be the same; I worried about my father's reaction and looked to Arty for answers.

"What do I tell my father? How do I break this horrific news? They were married for over fifty years; how will he react? My mother took care of him. How will he survive?" I rambled.

"Sit him down calmly, let him digest what you tell him, and we'll take it from there," Arty responded.

As we entered my father's house, he was preparing his dinner. The aroma of chicken soup filled the room bringing back memories of my mother's "cure all supper." How apropos, I thought. My father looked up.

"What brings you here? I called the airline and found out that mom's plane is delayed, so I decided to heat up my soup," he said.

"Dad, we have to talk to you. Come here and sit down," I said with Arty standing close by.

Looking at me curiously, he came over and sat down in his favorite oversized upholstered chair. I sat on his knee as if I was his little girl again, Tracy was at my side and Arty gripped my hand.

"Dad, something terrible has happened. Mom had a heart attack on the plane and died. She died in Jamaica, She's not coming home," my voice quivered as tears rolled down my cheeks.

My father looked straight ahead for a long time without moving. Was he in shock? Finally, he rubbed his eyes, reached for his handkerchief, blew his nose, and then asked for the details. I told him what I knew. I hugged him as we all sat together in silence.

The funeral arrangements were unusual, since we first had to get her body home from Jamaica. My boss at the Bahamas Tourist Office was helpful, as he knew the procedures for handling a death in a foreign country. Arty worked closely with him to expedite the process.

Two days after my mother's death, her red oversized suitcase arrived at my house, minus the portable luggage carrier, making the reality of her death even more painful. It sat in my dining room for a few days until I had the courage to open it. When I finally did, my hands shook as I unbuckled the worn straps. I opened it slowly; I didn't want to see her stuff, I wanted to see her! I hesitated to open the top of the suitcase and gazed at the ceiling as if I were looking for God's help. Taking a deep breath I looked down at the worn piece of baggage again then slowly opened it. Placed neatly on top of her clothing was a letter addressed to me that she had never sent. Clearly someone else had packed her bag and positioned the letter strategically. I wept as I opened the envelope and began to sob when I saw a photo of her sitting on a Jamaican bamboo raft, in her lime green bathing suit, wearing a straw hat. The caption on the souvenir photo read, "Rafting on the Martha Brae River, February 25, 1981." As difficult as it was for me to see these pictures, her smile showed that she had had a good time on her vacation, and that made me happy. My tears blurred the words as I tried to read the letter, "Dearest Children, I am having a wonderful time..." I couldn't continue; I had to stop, the pain was too great. Placing it back in the suitcase, I carefully looked through her belongings, and managed a smile when I saw the souvenirs for the kids: replicated bamboo rafts (small editions of the one she sat on in the photo) and Jamaican tops made from coconut shells. There were also two hand-carved birds that sit on my bookshelf to this day, their beaks pointing toward the sky.

In the Jewish religion, we bury the dead within twenty-four hours and sit Shiva (a period when family members and friends pay their respects) for the week following the funeral. In this case, we had no choice; we received visitors for a week and on the seventh day we had her funeral. Arty gave a poignant eulogy speaking of my mother's idiosyncrasies and her specialty foods; how she would dilute orange juice with water to make it last longer, calling it a "drink" instead of a juice, and her famous chicken soup in which she added bullion cubes to boiling hot water supplementing it with vegetables and potatoes to make up for what was lacking. Describing her plans to travel to China, Arty emphasized it was China's loss. I wept as he spoke.

I remember the snow falling as they lowered her casket into the ground and thought about the 60 degree weather the day she died. I wondered if this had a meaning; was my mother telling that me she had had a good time? Was she smiling down at us, letting us know that she controlled her destiny? My mother was always late—and she was late for her own funeral.

It was two days after we buried my mother and I thought I had closure. But soon the reality of not seeing her ever again set in. In my daughter's room, placing her pink and white checkered quilt upon her bed, I felt faint. My knees weakened beneath me and my body suddenly dropped to the floor. I called out for Arty. Rushing to my aid, he picked me up and carried me to my bed.

"I'm calling Mr. Hirsch. You need help," he said.

I nodded. We set the appointment for that afternoon.

Arty supported my weight as we climbed the two flights of stairs to Mr. Hirsch's office, and he waited for me in the waiting room. I sat in the familiar black leather chair and spoke about my mother, trying to understand why my body had an unwillingness to move and my mind had an acute lack of mental alertness. My mind and body had become enemies again, I thought. I rambled and once again, looked to Mr. Hirsch for a solution.

"You lost your best friend. Your mother gave you her unconditional love, and nothing and no one can replace that," he said with compassion. "You must allow yourself to mourn her death. In time you will heal, but know that her spirit will always be with you."

- ♪ ♪ ♪ -

Three weeks after my mother's death, I returned to work at the Bahamas Tourist Office. Still mourning, it was difficult to get back into a routine. I remember riding the bus, observing people, and thinking "why are these people alive when my mother is dead?" I tried to think of something else, something that would remove this empty feeling, something that would help fill the void.

I comforted myself with food and drink and quickly gained twenty-five pounds. Arty and I sat at a local eatery every Monday evening in the city, enjoying our cocktails, carving cheese from the big chunk of Jarlsburg resting on the bar. Knowing I was still in a lot of pain, he spoke to me one evening with concern in his voice.

"You're good at what you do—so you should use the Bahamas as a way to lessen your grief and help you to heal. Selling this travel destination promotes pleasure, happiness, laughter, relaxation, and transports people to a place of euphoria," Arty said. "So allow yourself to live vicariously through the people you help. I think this will help make you feel less hurt over time."

Listening to him intently, I thought, he's right. I must help myself and take control of my life; the wonderful memories will sustain me.

The following week, I drafted a monthly action plan. With the Bahamas offering so many options, I created a monthly calendar and titled it "Theme of the Month." I figured that the agents could use these themes to spur client interest.

The month of April came first, and I dubbed it my "Scuba Diving Month." I visited agencies and promoted scuba, making agents aware of the Bahama's coral reefs, shallow waters, and over 700 islands to choose from.

I called May my Nightlife and Entertainment Month. Painting a picture of the excitement of the casinos and shows, I told my customers, "The Bahamas is a mini Las Vegas. You don't have to travel as far to get there and to top it off, you have the Island's beautiful beaches to choose from."

June was the month for honeymoons. I advertised our packages, especially to the family of Out Islands, that offered romance, beautiful beaches, and idealistic hotels.

Summer was targeted toward families, and we offered affordable rates, putting particular focus on the activities for the kids, including the festival Junkanoo.

With each month that passed, so did my grief. Soon I felt more confident and back in my groove.

- ♪ ♪ ♪ -

Time passed quickly and after more than four years at the BTO, my job started to feel routine to me. Nothing had changed. I was still reporting to the same Manager and I wanted a promotion. I knew I deserved one. So I met with the District Sales Manager, and to my disappointment, learned that there was no place for me to grow in the company. Even after all my accomplishments and documented success, the politics of a government agency would not allow for a non Bahamian woman to be promoted to a more responsible position. Once I understood this, I handed in my resignation. Still, I was grateful for the experience, since it was my time at the BTO that allowed me to gain the knowledge and skills in marketing, sales, and public relations that exposed me to many new possibilities and opportunities in my business career. It wouldn't be the last time that the spirit of the Junkanoo would influence my life. The skills I learned at the BTO would later contribute to some of my greatest achievements.

- ♪ ♪ ♪ -

Quickstep

*The Quickstep is an international style
ballroom dance similar to a fast Foxtrot.
The dance originated in England in the 1920s.
Dancing a sixty second Quickstep
is equal to running a mile in record time!!*

From The Bedroom To
The Boardroom

Yearning for a new career option, it was a "quickstep" to working with Arty and dining with the President of the United States.

_I_n the spring of 1985, I settled in back at home. After working full time for five plus years, I had some difficulty adjusting. I enjoyed time with the kids, helping them with school projects, and my evenings were filled with wonderful meals as Arty and I dined regularly at local restaurants. One of our favorite restaurants was Buona Cucina; it even had a piano bar where we enjoyed singing songs like; _"New York, New York," "Fly Me To the Moon,"_ and _"Unforgettable."_ I delighted in watching Arty rest his arm on the upright piano, and with glass in hand, he crooned as if he were Frank Sinatra or Nat King Cole. To my amazement he even attracted a crowd. As regulars, we knew the entire staff; they were like family and treated us as such, but as much as I enjoyed these evenings and the quality time with my kids, I still itched for a new challenge.

My summer that year was peaceful, too peaceful. The kids were out of the house; Mitchell was working at a local clothing store and Gary was working at Baskin-Robbins; Kenny and Tracy were at camp, and the house had an empty quietness that amplified my restlessness. I started reading the help wanted ads in the *New York Times* researching marketing and sales positions, but then thought: Do I really want to do this again?

No, I thought, I want to do something completely different; but what? Putting the newspaper down, I took a sip of my coffee and stared at my brightly colored, yellow kitchen wallpaper with large blue flowers. I looked out my dinette window. Deep in thought, my mind drifted and new ideas filled my head. Recalling that I had once wanted to be a teacher, I remembered my first and only year at NYU's School of Education, which resulted in a summer job as a reservationist for Hilton Hotels, my first introduction to the world of tourism. Excited by embarking on this new career, I chose to work in travel rather than complete my college education; something I had always regretted, but never admitted.

Do I really want to teach? The word NO echoed in my mind. But getting a college degree excited me; to the point that I got up off my chair, threw the newspaper in the air, and paraded around the kitchen as if I were holding the NYU torch trying to remember the alma mater song. My head was clear, and my instinct told me to go back to college—not to become a teacher, but to become a shrink! That's it, I thought, I'll become a shrink. Visualizing myself like the cartoon character, Lucy from Peanuts, I'd hang out my shingle, "The Doctor Is In," and I'd save the world.

Based on my days as a "pseudo shrink" with people seeking out my advice and being in therapy myself, I knew the drill and understood the process. I laughed as I whispered Dr. Levy under my breath and relished in the idea of helping people to overcome their insecurities as I had overcome mine.

Excited by the possibility of my new career, I registered for a psychology class at Nassau Community College. Keyed up, I entered the college bookstore, and after I purchased the required reading, I treated myself to decals for my car and a hooded college sweatshirt with Nassau Community College embroidered with bold letters across the front. I felt as if I were eighteen years old, not forty-five.

Entering class, I nodded my head as if to say hello to the professor, wanting to be sure he knew I was there, and slid into a seat with an attached writing table that had remnants of past students' graffiti etched on it. Noticing the professor's name written on the blackboard, I took out my notebook and diligently wrote the date and his name on the first page.

The small classroom had four windows with white venetian blinds; the two middle blinds opened fully, the others were pulled up half way. The walls were painted a pale green. How apropos, I thought. Aren't psychiatric wards pale green? For an instant, I was reliving the movie, *One Flew Over The Cuckoo's Nest*. I felt like Nurse Ratched, or was her name "Nurse Wretched," wearing her pointed nurse's cap and starched white uniform parading around the wards checking charts. Shaking my head, I continued to drift. No, I couldn't be like her, she challenged and intimidated the inmates. I want to be a shrink, not a dictator. I laughed inwardly at my crazy thoughts.

Hearing the professor's voice, I brought myself back to the present and sat straight up, giving him my undivided attention.

"Good afternoon, I'm Professor Adams. Let's start with attendance, and then I will cover the syllabus for the semester," he said.

Excited when he called out my name, I answered in an extra loud voice, making sure he knew I was there.

After checking the attendance, he instructed us to open our textbooks and proceeded to explain variables versus non-variables. Trying to make his lecture more visual, he wrote on the blackboard, but all I saw were arrows, arrows resembling spears pointing to the left, the right, toward the ceiling and toward the floor. I had no idea what he was trying to convey. It was as if he were speaking and writing in a foreign language; there was no way I understood the deviation of a species from normalcy. What's normal? I thought. The concept was far too abstract for me to grasp. Adding to my exasperation, he announced we'd be tested at the end of this first week. With a quiz dangling over my head and my inability to seize the concept he was teaching us, self-doubt enveloped me. I hated the class and my self-doubt and assuaged my frustration by quitting the course after four days. I consoled myself by saying I had been a shrink for four days and had decided against becoming a Nurse Ratched.

Still, I struggled with the fact I would not be getting a college degree. Why should I even continue going to college, I thought. I have a degree; a degree in life experience! Raising four kids, overcoming major anxieties, and building a successful business career, I felt that I should have been awarded more than a degree. I should have been awarded a medal of honor!

Balancing precariously on the two rear legs of my kitchen chair, I gazed out the window. I questioned my talent and felt a bit unstable. I was afraid I'd return to an unhealthy state.

"What are you doing?" Arty asked as he entered the kitchen and opened the refrigerator.

I let out a loud squeal. "You startled me, don't do that," I shrieked as I thrust my chair forward, landing on all four legs.

Oblivious, Arty made himself a peanut butter and jelly sandwich. He sat down next to me and said, "I'm taking a lunch break. Are you hungry?"

Having recently opened his own accounting practice, Arty was preoccupied. So how could he know that I was struggling?

"No, food is the last thing I want. I want a job. I want a new career. What am I going to do? I need a purpose. Do you have any suggestions?" I asked him.

Taking a bite of his sandwich, he said without hesitation, "Why don't you come and work with me?"

My eyes widened and my mouth fell open. Was I imagining what he said? In disbelief I questioned him. "Work with you? What would I do? I don't know anything about accounting." My hands grabbed the table's edge.

Arty lifted my hands from the table and held them in his. He looked me straight in my eyes and said, "I'm not joking, I need help. You'd be great. Who better to come help build my practice than you? I already have a job for you—transform Mitchell's bedroom and make it into an office."

I got up and sat on his lap giving him a soft kiss. "You're my savior. When do I start?"

In the fall of 1985, Arty and I began working together. Arthur D. Levy & Co. was "our" company. I changed our son's room into an office, bought a computer, and set up shop.

Following Arty's orders, I purchased office supplies, organized the desk, answered phone inquiries from existing clients and prospects, and learned how to use the computer. Arty took the time to teach me how to enter income and expenses in a journal for our personal finances—it was my first introduction to basic bookkeeping. I wasn't a financial wizard, but I found this new task to be interesting. I looked for ways to summarize transactions, separating the personal from the business, and saving us money on taxes.

I loved to network and used this innate talent to attract new business, only at this time in my life I still hadn't recognized the scope of my skill. I thought I was just being social. I remember taking my kids for their first tennis lesson at the local indoor courts. After checking in at the reception desk, I looked around the waiting area and noticed a short, boyish-looking man wearing a navy and yellow warm up suit with "Team Tennis" written across the back of the jacket. I wanted to know more about the program and went to introduce myself. He welcomed my questions and told me he'd been teaching about ten years and had recently opened "Team Tennis."

I saw that as my cue. He was a new business owner, and I figured he must need an accountant. I told him about Arty and how we could help.

"I *do* need an accountant," the pro said. "Can you have your husband call me later this week?"

I had just sold our accounting services to my kid's tennis pro. Wow! I had chutzpah. If I could convince him, I could persuade almost anyone, I thought. My confidence soared.

I realized that I had created my own role within our business. Arty didn't have to rescue me. With our new partnership, our relationship continued to flourish, as did our business.

- ♪ ♪ ♪ -

Not long after we opened ADL & Co, Arty ran into an old colleague, Jim, who specialized in forensic accounting for divorces. Arty was intrigued by this specialty and started a discussion about merging. Our business was growing nicely with new clients filtering in everyday. I was not happy about the possibility of a merger.

One day after breakfast, as I drank my coffee, I questioned his decision.

"Why give up control and be accountable to a partner other than me? We are building a good business together; I don't want any other partners."

Sticking his head out from behind the newspaper, Arty answered without hesitation, "I want to bounce ideas around with someone who understands the accounting business. I also like the idea of forensic accounting—it would be a way to be like Sherlock Holmes and uncover the true financial stability of the business owner. More importantly if I got sick and was unable to work, there would be no income. I want to protect our future," he said as he pounded his fist on the tabletop as if it were a gavel.

I had no choice. Arty had made his decision, so we joined

forces with Jim, his wife, and three of their employees. They moved into a new office in an industrial park on Eastern Long Island. I stayed home for three months, lonely and bored. I must be patient, I thought. Arty will find something for me to do—he always did, he was my rescuer.

Strangely, after a while, their business prospects faltered and Arty came to me.

"I don't know what to do. The business is not doing well. Jim waits for the phone to ring, and my rolodex has become my Bible. If we don't do something quickly, we'll be out of business," he said pacing the kitchen floor.

Unsure about how to react, I tried to console him. "Calm down, calm down. Let's think about our options. We worked together before, why don't I come work with you again? I can use my talent to market your new business with Jim."

Arty stopped pacing, and said, "That's it. I'll tell Jim about your exceptional marketing skills and you can become our Marketing Director." Arty met with Jim the next morning and filled him in on my background. Jim, who was unfamiliar with the marketing process, said he would consider hiring me, but insisted that I interview with him before he made his final decision. Instead of confronting him, Arty agreed to his request, and the date was set for the interview the following week.

The thought of an interview caught me off guard. Self doubt surfaced, and I momentarily questioned my ability.

Throwing my arms up in disgust, I screamed to Arty, "How could you give Jim the power to interview me and decide whether or not he wants to hire me? I am your wife and that should be enough to qualify my employment. Doesn't he trust you?"

Continuing to vent, I rattled on, but then suddenly my anger turned to laughter. It was as if someone had flipped a switch on my mood meter. The release was like an emotional cleansing and I burst out laughing. The thought of being interviewed by my husband was ridiculous. My body shook with laughter, and my head moved side to side as if I were a bobble doll. Tears of hilarity rolled down my cheeks.

Bewildered, Arty said, "What's come over you? Does this mean you agree to the interview?"

I caught my breath and nodded.

The interview, while logical, would be an awkward experience. I couldn't envision Arty treating me as an employee, yet I was particularly thoughtful in selecting the appropriate attire. I searched my closet, rapidly pushing one hanger into the next, laughing silently and thinking I'm the boss's wife—how can I take this seriously? But I did. I carefully chose a newly purchased, designer, red, knee length dress with a matching jacket. Wearing red gave me a sense of power and made me feel in control. Holding the dress on the hanger just beneath my chin, I glanced in the mirror for final approval. "Perfect," I thought.

The interview lasted half an hour and was conducted in the conference room which, had I not been familiar with it, could have been intimidating. It was a formal room with a large, oval, high sheen, mahogany table and twelve burgundy, upholstered, swivel chairs. The carpet, also burgundy, was plush and the artwork was oversized.

Sitting down, I held on tightly to the arms of the chair

with sweaty palms. Jim looked at his list of questions and in an authoritative voice asked, "Tell me why we should hire you? What are your goals?"

After clearing my throat, I stood up, looked first at Arty, then at Jim, and responded, "I have a plan." I felt as if I were mimicking Dr. Martin Luther King's famous, "I have a dream" speech. I allowed Dr. King's voice to resonate in my mind; it gave me the confidence to proceed.

I told Jim I had a short term goal. "I see us getting thirty new clients by the end of the year," I said. "This gives me six months to turn around Katz, Levy & Co. Our target markets are entrepreneurs who need our services to keep them fiscally sound and attorneys who will use us as experts for forensic accounting and mediating couples going through divorce."

"And how do you propose to target these markets?" Jim interrupted. "How can you assure us you can bring in this new business?" Arty sat silently, listening intently.

Realizing I had sparked Jim's interest, I said, "That's the fun part. We'll join trade organizations such as the Bar Association and the Chambers of Commerce where we can network with business owners as well as attorneys. Additionally, we'll submit articles to their respective publications on topical financial issues and arrange speaking engagements featuring you and Arty as guest presenters. This combination is guaranteed to bring in new business for the company."

Taking a deep breath, I sat down. Clasping my hands, I looked at Jim and then at Arty for reassurance. There was a long silence except for the tapping of Jim's Mont Blanc pen on the long list of questions he had written on a notepad. Was he going to ask me more questions? Or had he made his decision?

Jim stood up and walked slowly around the conference table. I surmised this was his way of making me sweat, or of showing he was the boss.

Jim circled the table and sat back down. "OK, OK, you're hired with one stipulation. You have six months to turn Katz Levy around, and at the end of that time period, you will be evaluated based on our numbers."

He reached across the table, shook my hand, and told Arty to draw up a contract. I breathed a sigh of relief when he left the room.

"Whew," I mumbled under my breath as I rubbed my sweaty palms together. I had established my place in Katz, Levy & Co., only this time I had carved my own path to success by having a plan. Feeling as if I had just won a mini marathon, I got up and hugged Arty.

I knew I did a good selling job, but I didn't dare expose my vulnerability. I equated accounting to mathematics, and math was not my best subject back in high school. Arty had tutored me in ninth grade algebra and had bribed me with a large stuffed tiger to get me to pass the final exam. How could I promote accounting services? Would I be able to do it? I thought, Arty's creative with numbers. It's an easy sell—we're not "bean counters." We're magicians.

Ironically, during my first networking luncheon as Katz, Levy & Co.'s marketing director, I sat next to a banker. Knowing bankers were financial wizards, I wiggled in my seat as I introduced myself to someone I immediately dubbed "Mr. Banker." I couldn't let my fear take over so I initiated the conversation with a warm smile and asked him, "What do you do?"

Mr. Banker was receptive and as our conversation continued he asked, "What type of client do you look for? What size of clients do you handle: $3,000,000, $6,000,000, or larger?"

For an instant, I panicked. He was asking me to speak about numbers. I took a deep breath and without hesitation said, "You must meet my husband. He'll give you detailed information about the size of the clients we're looking for. He's a great businessman, and I know you two can do business together."

Mr. Banker agreed to meet Arty. I immediately took out my Filofax and scheduled an appointment. I had accomplished my goal.

As the months passed, it was obvious that Jim's way of operating was to sit back in his office and wait for the phone to ring. He wanted no part of the speaking engagements or networking gigs I arranged. Arty, on the other hand, looked forward to becoming known as an expert in his field. He relished participating in every talk I booked for him and was quickly learning the value of networking. After one year, their differences ultimately caused the demise of Katz, Levy & Co.

- ♪ ♪ ♪ -

With the dissolution of Katz Levy, Arty and I started ADL & Co. again. But this time, we opened our doors as equal partners. Our respect for one another changed our dynamics. We were a team. Arty had taught me the business side of the business and I had taught him about marketing and networking. Emotionally we were connected and Arty's role as my caretaker was a thing of the past.

In June 1987, we re-opened Arthur D. Levy & Co., subletting office space in a law firm on Fifth Avenue in midtown Manhattan. Our new location didn't have the glitz of Katz Levy but it wasn't my son's bedroom either. What was important was that we had access to a conference room and all the other essentials necessary to conduct our business.

Arty's office was painted soft blue and had a ten foot ceiling, which made it look much bigger. The large window signified status. There was also a designated space on the left side of his doorway for a desk for his personal secretary.

I furnished his office with an oversized walnut desk, two light beige filing cabinets, and two upholstered brown side chairs. Adding some greenery, I placed a sizeable Ficus tree in the back right corner and displayed his framed credentials on the wall above his desk. As I admired my own handiwork, I smiled and thought to myself, I could have been an interior decorator.

My office, a small L-shaped alcove, was just across the hall from Arty's. I bought a light oak desk and computer table that fit as if they were custom made for the space. For warmth, I added two small ferns and hung posters depicting New York City's skyline.

The New York Chamber of Commerce and Industry was our main source for business. I felt confident as the marketing director of my own business and attended the Chamber's monthly networking events known as "Business Card Exchanges." I insisted that Arty be at the first exchange with me and instructed him to fill his pockets with business cards as I did. The event was held at the AT&T building on Madison Avenue & 54ᵗʰ Street (today it is called the SONY building). Walking up the steps of the subway, I looked up at the tall, rose-colored granite building in awe.

"Come on Arty," I said as we ran across the street. "I don't want to miss any of this."

Upon entering the grand atrium, Arty squeezed my hand, looked at me, and said, "What am I doing here? Are you crazy? I'm not going into that ballroom. There must be 500 people inside, and I don't know what to say. Who do I talk to? Who would want to talk to an accountant?" He tried to hide behind my much shorter frame. I grabbed his hand tightly and pulled him close.

Arty looked sheepish as he shadowed me to the registration desk where we picked up our name badges. I pinned Arty's badge to the lapel of his jacket and pinned mine to the pocket on my dress. As I whisked him into the ballroom, I told him "follow my cues."

Walking through the room, I felt the energy of the crowd— voices echoed softly with the exchange of dialogue. As I perused the badges searching for names of companies, my eyes widened and my level of excitement heightened.

"The room is filled with lots of prospects," I whispered in Arty's ear. "Look at the badges, graphic design firms, computer consultants, there are endless opportunities and we can service them all."

After I walked around the perimeter of the room, I stopped and introduced myself to a well-dressed man who wore a plaid sport jacket with an open collared shirt. His dark brown hair was slicked back with what I presumed to be Brylcream.

"Hello," I said, "My name is Rosann Levy and this is my husband Arty. We have an accounting firm, what business are you in?"

"I own a small printing business in Brooklyn, New York," the gentleman said as he handed me his business card.

After hearing what he did, I asked Arty to give him a business card and then filled him in on our services.

As the evening started to wind down, Arty's grip on my hand loosened. Placing our empty wine glasses on the table, we walked out of the room. As we left the building, Arty put his hand into his bulging pocket and pulled out a handful of business cards. "You're good," he exclaimed, patting me on my back.

Arty was praising me. I had yearned for praise from my father my whole life. In a way, it was as if my father's voice was telling me I was good. Squeezing Arty's hand and filled with happiness, I pushed the revolving door and repeated silently to myself, I'm good.

Arty and I were active members in the Chamber of Commerce, but I was more visible because Arty handled the day to day work at the office while I continued networking to attract new business. I was so involved with the Chamber of Commerce events that people thought I worked there. I attended every card exchange, co-chaired the Networking Committee, and conducted networking breakfasts, during which small business owners presented their products or services before small groups. My days were filled with breakfast or lunch meetings, during which I developed relationships with prospects and touted our services. I remember one breakfast meeting with a woman who owned a travel agency. After a preliminary conversation we began to speak about our husbands and learned that they had similar personalities. They both liked sports, cigars, and good scotch. By the end of the meal, we arranged to go out on a dinner date—just the four of us. This was the beginning of a long and wonderful friendship. I signed them on as clients too.

Every week we were bombarded with an outpouring of new clients. The buzz about ADL & Co. in the business community caused a ripple effect, keeping Arty busier than ever meeting deadlines, preparing tax returns, and maintaining client satisfaction.

In 1987, corporations were downsizing due to an unstable economy. Many employees who were given early retirement or terminated opened their own small business and joined the Chamber. The outcome of layoffs added to my success as a networker since they were all in need of accounting and business consulting services. Most large firms refrained from taking on new entrepreneurs as clients, because they didn't think that they would be able to pay steep accounting fees. My presence at the Chamber led these kinds of businesses to us and Arty thrived on working with entrepreneurs—I suppose because he was an entrepreneur himself.

The frenzy in the marketplace sparked me to do more, and I expanded my networking to focus on women in business. I was elected President of the National Association of Women Business Owners for the New York Chapter. Again, since large accounting firms had no interest in taking on women business owners as clients, our business flourished with the addition of these entrepreneurial women clients.

One of the highlights of my labor of love was the bit of fame we enjoyed. We had numerous TV gigs, including appearances on the

Today Show, radio interviews on major stations, and feature articles in newspapers like *The Wall Street Journal* and *Crain's New York Business* and national magazines like *Fortune* and *Entrepreneur*. We were even honored by the Chamber and the Small Business Administration for our commitment to New York City and small businesses. Our newly found acclamations made me proud, and I created the ADL & Co. "Wall of Fame." As clients came into our office, they could see evidence of our accolades—the display of framed articles and notoriety jazzed up the hallway walls.

Within two years, we outgrew our sublet and rented our own space, two floors up. My interior design hat came into play again as we built out our new space. This time Arty's office had two floor-to-ceiling windows signifying even greater prestige, and we added an octagonal oak conference table. I took the middle office. The sun shone through my large window as if it were smiling on me. My confidence level was high and I felt as if my demons had finally left me.

As entrepreneurs, we were faced with new decisions daily. They included when to hire or fire an employee, buy or lease a copy machine, or invest in a postage meter. Arty agreed to everything with the exception of the postage meter. Licking stamps gave me a sticky tongue and my mailing list was growing. Still, Arty resisted the idea.

"Why do we need to spend the money on a postage meter, just get a sponge and dip it into a dish of water," he said looking for a small dish from the cabinet. After an arduous discussion, I won. "Mr. Pitney Bowes" glowed triumphantly in the mailroom.

Arty and I had different personality styles. We fit the "opposites attract" mold perfectly; he was laid back and I was type A. These differences, however, sometimes caused conflict when we tried to separate the bedroom from the boardroom. Often I wanted to talk business when we got home, but Arty would shut me down and tell me the office was closed. On the other hand, I'd sometimes make impulsive decisions about attending trade shows and other networking events without giving thought to a marketing budget. Arty was in a rage when I unilaterally signed us up for a booth at the New York Restaurant Trade Show.

"Do I have to put a leash around your neck? Taking a booth is over our budget. You can't keep spending money without talking to me," he said angrily as he slapped his fist on the desk and stormed out of my office.

We also had very different biological clocks. Arty was a morning person and I was a night owl. He'd get to the office by 8:00 a.m. I'd arrive between nine and ten. By 6:00 p.m., he was tired. I remember one of our biggest fights was when he wanted us to leave the office and go out together for a nice dinner, while I wanted to finish my mailing. That particular evening he came into my office and said, "It's 6:30 p.m., let's go."

I looked at him and said, "I'm not ready. I have to finish this month's mailing—it should take me about an hour."

Angry at my indifference to his feelings, Arty began to yell at me as I continued to stuff envelopes. Thank God I had "Mr. Bowes." Arty was normally not a screamer, but this night he blew up. He picked up a stack of envelopes and threw them on the floor. This was one of our more animated fights—we both paced the floor throwing up our arms in rage, along with anything that wasn't nailed down. Suddenly we realized how irrational we were being and started laughing. Calming down, we opened a bottle of wine and sat on the floor. We apologized to each other as we intertwined our arms and clicked our glasses together. After taking a sip, we kissed. I finished the mailing the next day.

After we were settled in our new office, Arty and I took a weekend off to spend time with friends in Woodstock, New York. Building a business was a challenging task, and we needed some time to recharge. My navy pea coat kept me warm as I sat on the patio sipping my morning coffee. The combination of the crisp mountain air and the logs burning in the newly built fire in the fireplace filled me with happiness. It was a beautiful day in the late fall. The sky was powder blue with clouds that looked like balls of cotton. The leaves had changed, and many of them covered the ground. Looking around at the mountains, I wondered about the famous concert in Woodstock and the chaos of the time—there was no chaos now—only peace and quiet. I glanced at Arty. His facial muscles were soft, telling me he was relaxed. He had a slight smile as he read the sports section of the newspaper. His team must have won, I thought.

My mind wandered as I drifted back in time to my childhood. I remember yearning for attention, yearning to be loved, yearning for a close family connection. The fear of my father's disapproval had left me scarred, the rejection from my siblings had made me lonely.

I thought about my children. My kids were my blood. They were my very heart and soul. Mitchell was a successful, recently married bankruptcy attorney. Gary was working at a midsize accounting firm in New York City. He had passed the CPA exam and had earned an MBA from Pace University. Kenny was attending New York City Technical College, majoring in hospitality management, and Tracy was a sophomore in Barnard College, majoring in English. They were setting out on their own paths to success but how could I keep them close? I wondered if any of my friends' families had close ties; none came to mind. The only families I could relate to were the families portrayed in TV sitcoms, like The *Brady Bunch*. Our family and the fictional Brady's shared some similarities—Gary's middle name was Peter and he looked just like him, so much so that he was called Peter by the campers when he went away for the summer during his teen years. The Brady's, like my kids, loved to play pranks. Of course my kids didn't neatly resolve their arguments in thirty minutes.

Suddenly I hit on it. Gary was a CPA. He could come and work with us. This was a way to keep at least one of my kids close to home, and close to me. This might fill the void inside of me left from the abuse and rejection of my childhood, I thought. I practically jumped out of my seat with exhilaration, but didn't want my hosts to think I was crazy. I contained myself until I had a chance to speak with Arty privately.

The remainder of the weekend was spent walking around the quaint town, enjoying country foods and wines, and shopping for unusual gifts made by local artists. Saying our good byes to our hosts, we embraced and thanked them for their gracious hospitality.

"What a beautiful weekend. I love the country, the fresh crisp air. I feel renewed," I said as I looked in the visor mirror blotting my lipstick. "How do you feel?"

Slowing down, Arty quickly looked to the left as we merged onto the Thruway. "I feel very relaxed for the moment," he responded as he accelerated the car.

Cruising at 65 miles per hour, I looked out the window, watching the open countryside fade away into the horizon. I wanted to read, but I found it impossible to concentrate. The monotone voice of the sport's reporter on WFAN radio lulled me into a meditative state. I closed my eyes and thought about Gary. He was a sweet, loving, spirited child—ala the cartoon character Curious George. Like the fabled monkey, Gary's deep brown eyes always seemed to glisten with sparks of mischief. In fact, I remember once parking my car on an incline and running into a convenience store to buy a quart of milk, leaving Gary, who was three years old, alone. "Curious Gary" pulled on the shift and caused it to go into reverse, so that the car careened down the hill into a busy intersection. God must have been watching, because the school crossing guard quickly opened the door on the driver's side and pulled Gary out of the car to safety. I realized that it was inexcusable for me to leave my son in the car while I bought a quart of milk. According to today's standards, I could have been arrested for child neglect.

Gary's crazy antics continued well into his teen years. From painting the hallway walls with graffiti in elementary school to scaling down a rope from his third floor bedroom window to escape my wrath because he didn't clean his room to constantly being called to the principal's office in high school for disrupting class, Gary was always up to some sort of mischief. I always wondered, what would be next for him?

Despite his mischievous acts, Gary was an achiever. While he was in high school, after passing his ocean test in the rough waters of the Atlantic, Gary got a job as a lifeguard at a well-established beach club. He kept this job until he entered his freshman year at Monmouth College in New Jersey. There Gary's grades excelled, and he was accepted at SUNY Albany where he completed his undergraduate education, graduating magna cum laude. We were proud of him, and when he tossed his graduation cap in the air, admittedly relieved.

Slowly I came out of my trance. I looked over at Arty who was still listening to the "Fan," his favorite radio station.

"You were sleeping," he said as he lowered the volume.

"No, no, I was in a daze, I was thinking about Gary."

I gave myself an opening. Shifting my weight in the seat, I sat up straight. I didn't know why I thought Arty would oppose my idea, but I felt that I had to do a good job selling him on the idea. I cleared my throat.

"Arty, we need help. The business is growing rapidly." I paused and took a deep breath. "Don't you agree?"

Nodding his head, yes, he looked at me. "What are you trying to say?"

"Being in the country this weekend has opened me up to new ideas about building our business, and I believe Gary is the answer— he has his CPA, his MBA, and most importantly, he's our son!"

My heart raced as I turned toward Arty. He made all the business decisions, so I knew he had to agree with my suggestion for it to work. He continued to drive in silence.

Changing lanes, Arty pulled to the side of the road and stopped the car. Shutting off the radio station, he turned to me and said, "I would like nothing more than to have Gary come into our business, but I have concerns about our financial stability. We are still a young company, and I'm not sure we can afford him. I don't want to put him at risk."

Clearly, he was conflicted. I could see he wanted Gary to join us in the business as much as I did. I tried to soothe Arty's fear. "Aside from his degrees, Gary's knowledge and expertise can help take our business to the next level—his computer and IT skills alone are invaluable," I said. "And if it doesn't work out with us, he can always get another job."

Leaning his shoulder against the car door, Arty put his hand to the side of his head. "I'm thinking about it, just give me a minute to digest all of this."

By the time we arrived home, we had decided that we would approach Gary the next day and make him an offer. We never had to, since Gary approached us first.

- ♪ ♪ ♪ -

"Mom, Dad, I've accepted a job at one of the Big Eight accounting firms, but I don't start until June," Gary told us the next afternoon when he stopped by our office on his lunch break. "I want to leave my job immediately and come to work with you until my new job begins. Is that OK with you?"

Gary swiveled in the chair as he continued to talk. "I'd be a big help to the company during tax season: I'll upgrade your computer system, teach you the new tax software, and implement better management systems. Just look at your desk piled high with returns," he said pointing to the mounds of paper.

With smiles on our faces, Arty and I asked him in unison, "When can you start?"

Shaking Gary's hand, Arty gave him a hearty pat on his shoulder and I hugged him. We immediately planned for Gary's temporary entrance into the family business.

In January of 1988, Gary joined Arthur D. Levy & Co. I smiled as I arranged flowers in a vase on the reception desk and attached six Mylar balloons that read "Welcome." As a little boy, I remembered that Gary had always loved balloons.

Gary shared Arty's office and set up the octagonal conference table as his desk. Overcome with joy, I watched him arrange books, a calculator, and his computer on his work station. Sitting in close proximity to Arty, I thought that he could be mentored by his father and at the same time learn firsthand the ins and outs of the business.

Once he was settled in, Gary met with Arty and laid out a plan that included weekly staff meetings (we had four employees) and a new system for reporting. He also made recommendations that we either upgrade our computer system or buy two new computers.

"I'll buy the new tax software and teach everyone in the office how to use it. It's a much more efficient way to prepare tax returns and it's faster too," he said as he placed an accounting pad on his desk. "Think of me as the quarterback," he said as he stood back pretending to throw a football to Arty. "Go out for a pass," he said laughing.

Arty and Gary's interactions touched me to the core. Their bond as father and son was enhanced now that they were business partners. As his mentor, Arty taught Gary the consulting side of our practice, like how to maintain quality service, how to negotiate, and how to value a business and problem solve. In turn, Gary showed Arty how to become proficient on the new computers and how to become adept at using the latest tax software. Saddened at the thought of Gary leaving us in a few months, I had to come up with a plan to make him stay. Gary was happy with us but the thought of working at what was then one of the Big Eight, excited him. I needed something that would guarantee that he'd stay. As if God was watching me, the opportunity came.

"Arty, Arty, " I shouted happily running into his office waving an invitation from the Chairman of American Express, who also happened to be the Chairman of the New York Chamber. "We've been invited to a luncheon at the New York Hilton with the newly elected President George H. W. Bush."

"Look, it has the Presidential seal," I said pointing to the invitation excitedly. "It's addressed to Gary, you, and me. I'll accept for the three of us."

I hadn't shunned my liberal politics, but I certainly couldn't pass up the chance to meet a sitting President.

I wanted us to stand out in the crowd for this milestone, so I instructed Arty and Gary to wear their finest attire.

"Maybe the President will notice us," I said straightening

Arty's tie. "Be sure to put a hankie in your left breast pocket that coordinates with the color of your shirt," I told them. "Pink or blue would be a good choice. You both look good in either of those colors."

Arty and Gary looked at each other while rotating their pointer finger towards their heads as if to say I was crazy. Ignoring them, I left clutching the invitation like a prize.

Security was extremely tight as we arrived at the hotel. Broad shouldered men stood in every possible corner holding walkie talkies and wearing ear pieces. They directed us through rows of blue draped corridors and metal detectors. After passing though our last security check, we quickly followed the herd of people toward the Grand Ballroom. Upon entering the room, I instantly felt the energy of the crowd. The assemblage was corporate New York— men wearing blue pin striped suits and women wearing Ann Taylor dresses. I heard the clink of ice cubes in glasses as people walked around networking and looking for seats; there was no reserved seating. Gary headed toward the stage area where a podium was set up with teleprompters on both sides. We followed Gary. Seated directly in front of the podium, I noticed Gary scanning the room and watched as he fixated his eyes toward the curtain to the left of the dais. Suddenly a man's voice announced,

"Ladies and gentlemen, please welcome the President of the United States!"

The ballroom was filled to capacity and over 2000 people stood up and applauded when the President and Mrs. Bush entered. I never forgot that moment.

"We're dining with the President of the United States," Gary said while buttering a roll. "I can't believe it—I'm actually sitting in front of the President!"

Just before dessert was served, the President was introduced again and stood at the lectern to a standing ovation. Gary turned his chair to face the President. Crossing his legs, he sat back and gave his full attention to every word spoken. President Bush talked with sincerity about his Presidential theme "1000 Points of Light" and a "kinder, gentler nation," two catchphrases coined by his speechwriter. After his speech, guests lined up at the microphones which were placed on both sides of the room and asked questions. After answering the questions, the President thanked everyone and prepared to leave the dais. Gary was determined to personally meet the President, so he pushed his way through the mob of people, all vying for a handshake. First he shook hands with Mrs. Bush and then introduced himself to the President. Astonished, I watched my son converse with the President of the United States as I held my breath and covered my mouth with my hand. I mused that our lives had certainly been in Quickstep mode for a while. I wondered if the fast pace would continue, or would it be stepped up even more than it was now, if that were at all possible.

The following week, Gary mailed his resignation letter to Deloitte, Haskins & Sells.

- ♪ ♪ ♪ -

Bolero

*Bolero was a Spanish dance
that was introduced to the United States
in the mid-1930s. At that time, it was danced
in its classical form, which was performed
to the constant beat of the drums.*

Trouble In Paradise

**The constant beat of the Bolero drums
would be heard loud and clear
in the family business.**

*I*t was January 1989 and six months since Gary had joined us at the company. He was a good worker and had become comfortable in his role. But the once-pleasant work atmosphere changed as family issues started trickling into the business. Rather than thinking of us as business partners, he went back to being our son and lashed out if things didn't go his way.

"Any dummy can do it," I heard Gary say as his voice reverberated through the office. For a moment, I remembered my father's early reprimand and wondered, as I quickly ran down the hall, if Gary had heard my father use this phrase, or was it me he was mimicking?

Arty was sitting at the computer in his office staring at the screen while Gary stood over him, pointing to the screen. "Click the mouse twice and the Excel file will open," he told Arty and then he slammed a book on the desk, after which he walked away, shaking his head in disgust.

I followed Gary into the reception area. "He doesn't get it. I lost patience with him," Gary told me. "Let's hire an outside consultant to teach Arty how to use the Excel program. It's so easy, any dummy can do it," he repeated and turned to look out the window.

Every day there seemed to be another family feud brewing. I remember one day Arty took Gary to a new client meeting and returned from the meeting complaining to me about Gary's behavior. "Why did I take him? His performance was unacceptable." Although, usually Arty tried to control his emotions, today he was angry.

"Doesn't he ever learn?" Arty continued, as he propelled his arms forward as if striking a punching bag. "I don't know why he bothered to come. He yawned during the entire meeting, picked his fingernails, and was unresponsive to questions."

I sat behind my desk with my arms crossed and watched Arty pace my office with the intensity of a steamroller.

Motherhood took over. I stood up, walked in front of him, and held both my hands up as if they were a stop sign.

"Maybe Gary couldn't relate to the client because he was more like your peer than his," I said.

As Gary's mother, I was protective and made excuses, but as his business partner, I understood Arty's feelings. I was conflicted. Do I reprimand Gary or do I discuss the issue on a business level? I decided this was business, not personal, and confronted Gary.

"What happened during the meeting? Dad said you behaved poorly. Why?" I spoke as if I were about to give Gary a time out.

"Stay out of this," Gary responded. "I don't have to answer to you. Leave me alone, I'm busy." He jerked his body away from me, and went back to working on his computer.

I felt stuck in the middle.

But Arty and Gary weren't the only ones that battled. Gary and I had our share of fights too. I remember one argument we had about his choice of footwear.

"Gary, why are you wearing sneakers? Where are your shoes?" I asked pointing to his feet as he entered the office one morning.

"I'm more comfortable in sneakers. I'd go barefoot if I could. I only wear them en route and I change to my shoes when I have client meetings," he said tersely as he flipped through the pile of mail on the reception desk.

"Don't ignore me," I said, raising his chin up with my hand. "Look at me when I'm talking to you. You're a professional, and professionals do not wear sneakers to work. You wouldn't do this if you worked at Deloitte!" My body stiffened as I raised my voice.

Once again, Gary ignored me, shook his head, and walked past me to his office. Like a soldier, I turned and marched down the hall.

The ongoing hostility forced me to seek outside counseling, so I called Dr. Hirsch. He recommended that I make an appointment with Myra Watkins, a woman who had her doctorate in clinical psychology and specialized in family therapy. I made an appointment for the following week. Now, all I had to do was try to convince Arty and Gary to meet with a "shrink."

Later that morning, I was nervous as we sat around the conference table going over the schedule for the day. Beads of perspiration formed on my brow. Absent mindedly, I twiddled my thumbs. For a moment I felt like the Cowardly Lion from the *Wizard of Oz*. "Courage, courage," I mumbled under my breath as I patted away the sweat from my forehead. Impulsively, I blurted out, "I made an appointment with a counselor next week." I was careful not to use the word shrink. "She can teach us how to separate family issues from the business," I said folding my hands on the table. Prepared for a negative response, they surprised me by asking in unison, "what day and time?" I breathed a sigh of relief.

Dr. Watkins, a woman in her mid fifties with a petite frame and a pixie-like hair style that resembled Peter Pan, greeted us warmly when we entered her home office on Manhattan's upper west side.

"Hello," she said as she welcomed each of us with a handshake. "Come in and take a seat."

Her office was stark with four chairs grouped in a small circle around a glass top coffee table. There were two small grey herring-bone patterned swivel arm chairs, one high-backed leather chair, and a fourth one with a black metal frame. The walls were covered with photographs of her world travels and a miniature sculpture of Buddha sat on the sill of a large picture window overlooking Central Park.

Arty and Gary both raced for the high-back leather chair, which I surmised signified control. It was as if they were two little boys fighting over a toy. I laughed internally.

Dr. Watkins's was dressed simply in a long skirt, light beige knit sweater, and Birkenstocks. She was soft spoken, yet her tone demanded response. Our evaluation took two hours with each of us compulsively talking over one another. We discussed issues of control, respect, competition, and boundaries. She took notes on a yellow legal pad, flicking through the pages quickly to keep up with our loose tongues. Finally, Dr. Watkins interrupted our discussion.

"That's all for today. I'll see you back here next Tuesday and give you the results of my evaluation," she said as she lay her pad back down on the coffee table.

I was bewildered, since I had anticipated an instant solution. How would I get through the week? Shaking Dr. Watkins' hand I said, "Can't you give us a quick fix?"

"See you next week," she repeated, smiling and cupping my hand in hers. Something about her soothing touch released the tension between my shoulder blades.

The next week, at our session with Dr. Watkins, once again Arty and Gary raced for the high back chair. Arty got there first.

"Good morning," Dr Watkins said as she took her seat across from Arty. I swiveled around restlessly in one of the grey upholstered chairs and asked her, "Dr. Watkins, do you think we will stay together as a family in business?"

Smiling, she prefaced the session by saying that the data she collected told her we are a loving supportive family, but that our ambivalence created a lot of chaos.

"Your decision making process is clouded by constant opposition, confrontation, and feelings of uncertainty. There are too many chiefs and not enough scouts. Once you clearly define who's in charge and how to maintain boundaries amongst the three of you, the management of your office will run smoothly. You must implement change or the business will not grow, and more importantly it will continue to adversely affect the family dynamics," she said, as she leaned forward in her chair.

I uneasily swung my chair rapidly to the right, then to the left, looking at my husband and son for answers.

"And how do you propose we go forward?" Arty asked.

Dr. Watkins sat back. "Start by listening to each other. Don't talk over one another. Write out an agenda off premises for your weekly business meetings and in that agenda, frame out plans for the week ahead. These meetings will improve communication and clarify each of your roles," she told us, smiling warmly.

We did as Dr. Watkins suggested and met weekly at a coffee shop near our office. The first task on our list was to spell out job descriptions. We gave Arty the title of Managing Partner and made him in charge of the overall management, which included staff issues, workloads, and putting out fires, both internal and external. We had recently added three new employees, making our total staff ten, so this was the perfect position for Arty. Gary wanted carte blanche on all computer issues including the purchase of new software and training, so his job title was Director of Operations. My job was easier to define. As Director of Marketing, I only had to learn how to not interfere in matters that were not related to marketing. Our new, clearly defined roles served to improve our communication and our decision making process. We had a renewed respect for one another and our changed behaviors filtered into the now successful management of the firm.

We continued our sessions with Dr. Watkins every month for the next several years and found that they were invaluable. But one particular meeting stayed with me. Gary had been working with us for close to three years and he was newly married. Arty and I arrived early that morning. Not having to fight Gary off this time, Arty quickly took his seat in the high-back leather chair. Awaiting Gary's arrival, we made small talk with Dr. Watkins. When Gary came into the room his entrance took me by surprise: his head hung low and he dragged his feet as if he were carrying a heavy weight on his back. He took his seat in the metal framed chair. We sat in silence knowing something was very wrong.

"What's wrong?" I asked as I caressed his arm in hopes of making him smile.

His head still hung low, he began to speak. "As a newlywed, I'm still adjusting to married life. We're having fun, but we have no responsibilities other than to each other and have been thinking of moving to California. Also, I'm not sure if the family business is my future. I want to explore other options." He raised his head as if the weight was lifted and looked at Arty and then me.

My mouth dropped wide open. Arty just sat and stared into space. Then Arty stood up, walked toward the picture window, and with his back to us, began to speak slowly as if he were carefully choosing his words.

"Gary," he began, "I love having you work in the business with your Mother and I. The thought of you helping us build this business has been our dream. You are very good at what you do, and if you stay, I know you will take this business to a much higher level—the choice is yours." He paused for a moment, then continued. "No matter what your Mother and I feel, we want you to live your life based on what *you* want, not what *we* want. I would rather have you love me as your father than be angry at me as your business partner. You have our unconditional love regardless of what you do," he said his voice racked with anguish as he turned away from the window and took his seat.

My heart ached for Arty, as it brought back painful memories. I knew he'd do anything not to repeat the relationship he had with his father. He never wanted his kids to harbor resentment or feel rejected the way he had. I dug my fingertips in the arms of the upholstered chair. My fantasy of keeping the family together was turning into a nightmare.

Our session ended early and we left Dr. Watkins' office and headed back to our office. Arty and Gary limited their conversation to client matters. My head was pounding as if it had been hit with a wooden mallet.

"Anyone have a Tylenol?" I asked as I rummaged through my handbag.

Arty and Gary quickly shook their heads and continued their discussion. I was amazed at their indifference. How could they not be affected as I was? Was it because I was Gary's Mom and couldn't accept that my son could consider leaving me? In my mind, I repeated over and over, he can't leave...he can't leave...he can't leave. I arrived back at the office, folded my arms, laid my head down on them, and wept.

"Can I come in?" Arty asked, peeking through the open door. I grabbed a tissue and blew my nose into it. "Sit down," I said, "we need to talk."

Arty took a seat and gently reached over to smooth my disheveled hair away from my eyes.

"What are we going to do?" I asked pitifully, blowing my nose again.

"There is nothing we can do," Arty said, calmly sitting back in the chair and crossing his legs. "We must let Gary make his own decision and not force him to stay with us. We raised him to become his own person, and if he wants to fly, we can't stop him. We've done our job; the rest is up to him. Together we will continue to build ADL & Co., regardless of what happens with Gary."

I fixed my eyes on his. I knew Arty spoke the truth. I just had to come to terms with the possibility that Gary might leave. He had to live his life, as we had to live ours. Arty stood up and walked around my desk. He pulled me up and we hugged.

Logically, I understood the reality of the situation, but emotionally it was still hard to accept. I clung to Arty for several minutes. The warmth of his body relieved some of my pain. Kissing me on my cheek, he walked out of my office.

I sat back down behind my desk, rehashing our conversation. As I picked up a pencil and began to doodle, I remembered how my mother would say "what will be, will be" each time she was faced with obstacles in life. Even with her gone so many years, I felt that she was still teaching me lessons. "What will be, will be," I thought and picked up the phone to check on my messages. I smiled as I heard one of my potential clients ask me to set up a meeting for him with Arty.

Business went back to normal and ADL & Co. continued to grow steadily. We knew that Gary was a procrastinator, and thought that it would take him time to make his decision, so we didn't discuss the subject again. One month later, Gary came to us and said he had decided to stay. My fantasy of keeping my family close to me was a reality once again. And soon, our growing business would take us into a whole new enterprise.

- ♪ ♪ ♪ -

In the spring of 1992, I was invited to be a guest speaker at the annual conference for the American Association of Accounting Marketing Executives in San Francisco. My topic, "Networking, A Blueprint For Professional Survival" was a big draw. At the conference, a colleague approached me and suggested that I open a non profit family business organization as a marketing arm which would bring in a lot of new business for ADL & Co. He told me that their accounting firm incorporated such an organization in Chicago and that it had opened doors to a market that controlled 90% of the businesses across the country.

"What are you talking about? What's a family business organization? How can it attract new business?" I questioned as I nibbled on crackers and cheese and sipped white wine at the cocktail reception.

"ADL & Co. is a family business and that makes you credible. If you form an educational membership organization for families in business these kinds of companies will seek you out for your expertise. Hold monthly meetings with experienced guest speakers who focus on topical issues and you're guaranteed to corner that market in the Northeast," he told me as he poured himself a glass of red wine.

Excited by the idea of this new venture, I gulped my wine and searched the room for Arty. "Thanks so much for sharing your thoughts with me. I will put a plan together as soon as I get back to

New York. May I call you if I have any more questions?" I asked as I put my glass down and picked up a napkin to wipe my lips.

"Anytime," he said and handed me his business card.

As soon as we returned to New York I prepared a business plan for this new venture. Arty and I incorporated the Family Business Council of Greater New York (FBC) in October 1992. We appointed a board of directors, created the budget, and obtained corporate sponsors as underwriters that included Chemical Bank and IBM. Gary remained focused as Director of Operations for ADL, and we updated him on our progress at our regular weekly meetings.

Our first FBC meeting was held on February 4, 1993 at Chemical's corporate headquarters on Park Avenue in New York City. During the cocktail reception, I networked and after introducing myself to several family business owners that included husbands, wives, fathers, and sons, I met Mr. Herbert, owner of an eighty-year-old, third generation coffee roaster.

He smiled flashing his white teeth as he shook my hand and said without hesitation, "Hi. We are looking for a new accountant. Our CPA is retiring and we are interviewing now. Have your husband call me as soon as possible, as we will make our decision within one week."

He gave me his business card, and I told him to expect a call from Arty in the morning. As I put his card in my pocket, my confidence soared. After shaking a few more hands, I made my way to the podium. Standing in front of more than 100 people, I took a deep breath, smiled, spoke into the microphone, and said,

"Good evening and welcome. My name is Rosann Levy and I am the President and Co-Founder of the Family Business Council of Greater New York." I looked around the room as everyone applauded. I was in a dreamlike state and thought, Wow—I've just given birth to a new baby.

The FBC grew quickly and within six months we had more than 100 members. With each meeting, I heard our new member's family business sagas.

In one situation, a father working with his three children found out that one of them had goofed off. Calling his son into his office, he questioned his work ethic saying he had heard that his son had a habit of leaving the office early on Fridays, arriving late on Mondays, and all, without completing his workload. He then looked directly into his son's eyes and said, "Your lack of responsibility is inexcusable, so you give me no choice. You're fired!"

Having said that, the father turned around in his chair, put his hand to his head, looked back at his son, and said, "Son in the family business I wear two hats and now I am wearing the hat as your Dad." Then he said, "Son, I just heard you were fired, is there anything I can do to help?" The audience roared with laughter...and recognition.

During our second meeting, there was a heated discussion about what name the adult children should call their parents during office hours. In this particular case, the son refused to call his parents Mom and Dad and the parents refused to allow him to call them by their first names. They compromised and the son agreed to call them by their initials. I was shocked that this was a problem for many of the families. Gary had called us by our first names from his first day on the job, and we had never given it a second thought.

But one of the most painful stories we heard was a father

telling us that he had to fire his daughter-in-law because she was more qualified to run the business than his son. His son, an IT guy, hid behind his computer and was completely overshadowed by his wife. She established relationships with the employees, controlled daily work schedules, monitored inventory, and had become the face of the business. As his father, he intuitively sensed his son's emotional distress but couldn't confront him. Rather than continue to watch him suffer, he fired his son's wife.

On the lighter side we learned about the "talking stick."

"What is a talking stick?" one of our members shouted from the audience.

The speaker, a tall lanky balding man, smiled as he picked up a beautiful hand carved stick about the length of his forearm. Holding it in his hand he explained that the talking stick was originally used by North American Indians at council meeting as a cue for the rest of the council members to keep from interrupting the chief while he was speaking. When the chief finished, the talking stick was passed on to the next council member who wanted to speak.

"I brought this stick back from Vietnam, but it doesn't matter what kind of stick is used—it could be a pencil or an ice cream stick—it's what the stick represents," he said as he passed it around the audience.

The stories continued, and the FBC played an integral part in resolving a lot of the issues within these family businesses. Our expert speakers taught members to separate the family from the business, telling them to run the business with their heads and not their hearts. They taught our members about boundaries, control, how to hire and fire family members, and succession planning—the major issue in passing the business from generation to generation.

News of the FBC traveled quickly, and members joined daily. ADL & Co. benefited from the growing membership too. Gary continued to focus on ADL & Co., servicing existing clients and handling our growth. I was writing articles, managing new members, holding board meetings, planning monthly meetings, social events, and new member receptions. I was doing so much that I was at a breaking point. I felt overwhelmed and told Arty and Gary that I needed help.

"Contact the local college career centers to find students who are majoring in marketing," Gary suggested as he continued to download new software.

"I like that idea," said Arty, "and it won't cost us any money to advertise."

I laughed happily and walked down the hall to my office to draft a help wanted flyer. I had just finished printing out the flyer when my son Kenneth called.

"Hi Ken," I said proofing the flyer. "What's up?"

"I have a problem. Barbara doesn't want me to continue working at the restaurant. The hours are long and I get home late. As a newlywed, she wants me closer to home and I want to work closer to home too. I gave my resignation today, so I am looking for a job," he said almost stuttering.

I dropped the flyer on my desk and said, "You couldn't have called at a better time. I desperately need help with the FBC. How would you like to come and work with me?" I asked him grabbing the receiver tightly.

"Work with you? What would I do? My degree is in hospitality management. I only know the restaurant business," he said.

"You have great people skills—that's all you need to manage the FBC. You will develop relationships with the members, alert them to our events, and outreach for new members. I'll train you," I said. "Come on in and we'll talk about it."

Kenny met with me the next day and he started work the following week. My fantasy of keeping my family close to my bosom was growing. My "toy boy" was coming to work with me.

Since I wasn't thinking about Gary's reaction to the news of Ken joining the firm, I was surprised when he questioned my decision.

"You're still taking care of him," he said with disgust as he stood with his back to me and looked out the window. I wanted to defend myself, but decided to let Gary vent.

As he spoke, I remembered the difficult time Ken had growing up living in the shadow of his two older, macho brothers. He didn't have their physical strength, courage, or aggressiveness. Despite that, he continually looked for their acknowledgment, only to be shunned. His easygoing temperament changed dramatically in high school when he cut classes, neglected to turn in homework, and was a chauffeur for his friends earning him the moniker "king of the road."

"Are you listening to me?" Gary questioned as he put his hands on my shoulders and shook me out of my trance.

"Yes, yes, I hear you," I said, my voice going up an octave. "But you're wrong, I'm not taking care of him, he has a wife who can do that. I need help, and he's the perfect candidate," I said firmly, and walked away.

- ♪ ♪ ♪ -

I welcomed Ken into the company the following week. I didn't get balloons to greet him, like I had done for Gary, but instead I had framed posters of his favorite teams: the New York Mets, the New York Giants, and the Knicks hung on the wall. As I set up his special welcome, my mind drifted to the special bond Ken and Arty had always shared. Ken was Arty's buddy. As the last son to leave home for college, Ken was able to spend quality time with Arty without having to compete with his older brothers. However, Ken and Arty's obsession with professional team sports was the true link between their souls. To them, the seasons revolved around sports: fall/winter was football season, spring/summer was baseball season, and in between they rooted for the Knicks. I laughed silently to myself as I hung up the last poster and went to the reception area to welcome him.

Passing Gary's office, I stopped in and said, "Kenny's starting today, why don't you come and welcome him."

Gary waved his hand to the side, indicating no. I ignored him and continued walking toward the reception area. Arty joined me, and we greeted Kenny as he opened the door. I was so happy he was here that I pulled him toward me and gave him a big hug. Arty shook his hand, and then introduced him to the staff that was milling around the reception desk.

"Let me take you to your new office," I said, pulling at the sleeve of his suit jacket. I couldn't wait to see Ken's reaction to the life size posters of the famous sports legends I had hung up. I felt like I was giving a new toy to my little boy.

"OK, OK, I'm coming," he said picking up his briefcase. Arty tagged along.

Passing by Gary's office, Ken stopped to say hi. Gary was busy at the computer and grumbled hello, as he barely looked up. I was sad to see Gary's reaction. Attributing it to sibling rivalry, I chose to let it go and not make it an issue as Ken and I continued down the hall.

"Wow, you remembered all of my favorite players," Ken said as he entered the office. Pointing toward the football poster he said, "Phil Simms was awesome in the 1989 Super Bowl. I remember he set the Super Bowl passing record. Doesn't it still stand today?" he asked Arty.

"It sure does," Arty responded, pretending to throw a ball.

Arty and I stood by the doorway and watched Ken walk around his desk.

"This is great," Ken said. He sat down and turned on his computer.

"I left you a 'to do' list and if you have any questions, buzz number twelve on the intercom," I said and left, hand in hand, with Arty. I was overjoyed. Now I had two out of my four kids working in our family business.

Ken adjusted quickly to his new job. He coordinated all the FBC monthly meetings and new member receptions, developed relationships with members, and scheduled annual fundraising social events that included our golf and tennis outing, silent auctions, and our holiday party. I assisted him, but his ability to take charge freed me up to write monthly newsletters for both companies, attend industry specific trade shows for ADL & Co, and plan conferences for the FBC.

The formation of the FBC gave us creditability as experts in the family business market. Then a fantastic dining experience at Danny Meyer's new restaurant, Union Square Café, opened our doors to the hospitality industry. Arty and I had first enjoyed dining at this top rated restaurant not long after it had opened. Impressed by the restaurant's request for the customer's evaluation of their dining experience, I sent Danny Meyer our press kit telling him we were a customer-service oriented business too. Within a few weeks of receiving our material, Danny called and said he was looking for a new accountant. After interviewing twelve other accounting firms, Danny chose us and from that day forward we were known as specialists in the hospitality industry. Gary was the partner in charge of the ADL & Co. Hospitality Group. ADL & Co. and the FBC were becoming famous and growing rapidly.

Ken reported to me for most of his responsibilities. He reported to Gary only on work projects that were specific to the restaurant industry. This made their rivalry in the workplace inevitable. One day I was on the phone with my graphic designer when I heard Gary yelling at Ken. I knew I shouldn't intervene, but as their mom I was driven to break up the fight.

"I told you to call the representatives in Chicago, San Francisco, Phoenix, and Boston to get a head count for each workshop I was conducting," Gary screamed as he shook his fist at Ken. Gary ran workshops that focused on trends in the restaurant industry, and Ken's job was to make sure that these mini conferences were well attended. "Did you even make any of the calls?" he asked his brother.

Without waiting for an answer, Gary pounded on the desk. "The turnout is very light with the exception of San Francisco and Chicago. You're costing us money!" He brushed by me and stormed out.

Ken looked at me with his big blue eyes and shrugged his shoulders. I remembered him giving me the same look when he didn't complete his homework assignments in school. He always looked innocent—it was those beautiful eyes with the long blond lashes. I could never get angry with him. But this was business, and he wasn't a little boy anymore. It was time for him to take responsibility for his actions.

"Ken, did you make the calls?" I asked him pointedly. "I left them messages," he replied nodding. "I was waiting for their call backs; I guess I waited too long." He took a deep breath. "I'll explain everything to Gary when he calms down. Mom, please stay out of this. I'll resolve it." He went back to reviewing the list of reps he had in front of him.

Thankfully, these incidents didn't happen very often, and when they did I learned to mind my business and let my sons take care of it themselves. Our family therapist, Myra, helped too; she reiterated that I was not to cross boundaries. "You must learn to let your son's handle their differences. Protecting one son against the other creates rivalry," she told me. I was glad Myra reminded me to butt out.

- ♪ ♪ ♪ -

We received an invitation letter from Association for the

Advancement of Retired Persons (AARP) just as Arty was about to turn sixty. Annoyed, he threw it in the garbage, yet oddly enough, to save money, he applied for his senior citizen Metro card and bought senior tickets at the movies.

"It's only $1.00 to ride the subway and movie tickets are half price. Look how much money we're saving because I am old," he said, laughing. "Soon I'll collect Social Security and get my Medicare Card."

"You're not old," I said rubbing his back. "Age is only a number."

I always wanted to make him feel better and thought that I should do something extra special for his 60th—something that would make him feel young.

It was December 1998. Arty's 60th birthday was on February 12, 1999. I thought about his love of baseball and remembered that spring training began on February 1st. A friend had told me about a fantasy baseball camp that took place in major league training camps in Ft. Myers, Florida in January.

"It's a wonderful experience for anyone who loves baseball," my friend told me on the phone. "I went last year. I wore a New York Mets uniform and played competitively against other teams. To top it off, we were coached by retired professional ballplayers," he said, with excitement in his voice.

That's it, I thought. I'll surprise Arty and send him along with our sons to fantasy baseball camp. He can immerse himself in his very own fountain of youth!!

Arty left for baseball camp with his sons in mid January. He wore a Phillies uniform with his name imprinted on the back of the shirt, just as if he were a true pro ball player. He was coached by some of the greatest—Carl Yastrzemski, Frank Robinson, Brooks Robinson—and others. He came home with a group souvenir photos and the ball he hit that won the series in his league.

"The trip was awesome. I felt like I was in my twenties again," he told me as he stared at the picture of him sitting right in the center of some of baseball's best ball players.

Arty's pleasurable experience from baseball camp was short lived. It was the middle of tax season, and he was working long hours and weekends.

"I'm tired," he said as he went through the list of returns. "I don't know how much longer I can do this." He got up and paced the floor. "The clients are driving me crazy by constantly questioning me: Am I getting money back? Will I be audited? Can you put me on extension? Even more annoying is the fact that they never say thank you." He hesitated. "And we have a bigger problem. One of our staff accountants, who we hired two years ago, just gave notice. At least he's staying until the end of tax season." He sat back down and leaned his forehead in the palms of his hands.

"Arty, tax season is short. Let's plan a trip. We'll go after April 15th. You pick the destination and I'll book it," I said massaging the back of his neck.

"That's a great idea," he said, giving me a big smile.

We got through tax season and left on April 16th for a vacation in Italy—Arty's favorite destination. We had been to Italy once before and at that time had visited Rome, Florence, and Venice. This time we headed south and spent ten days on the Amalfi Coast—one of the most spectacular places on earth—where the mountainous coastline stretches south of Naples and picturesque fishing villages cling precariously to the cliffs. The winding roads challenged Arty's driving skills.

"I love this," he said as he shifted our rented Fiat into second gear.

"You must be Italian," I said clinging to the armrest. "They're crazy drivers too. Slow down and look at the scenery, it's breathtaking."

"If I look now, we'll be in the sea," he said as he revved the engine and took another curve. "This is fun!"

Looking at his child-like wide eyes and big smile, I let him be.

Sitting on the beachfront of the luxury San Pietro Hotel overlooking the Tyrannian Sea, we sipped Limoncello, a specialty liquor made from lemons that was native to the area. I glanced at the cascading foliage hugging the shoreline and watched as the waves broke gently against the rocks. We held hands as we watched the sun set and I leaned my head upon his shoulder. I thought, this is what heaven must be like.

We toured Pompeii, Sorrento, and the hillside village of Ravello where we bought local hand painted ceramic art. One of the highlights of our trip was an excursion to the Isle of Capri, known as the most beautiful island in the world. We set sail from Naples and watched Mt. Vesuvius melt into the horizon. Arty was so taken by the beauty of the island that he told me that when he died he wanted his ashes thrown into the sea just before the ferry pulls into the harbor.

"I can't promise that," I said as I stood on the bow of the boat and took in the sights of the fishing boats in the harbor. "You'd be too far away from me."

He laughed, as he put his arm around my waist and patted me affectionately on my butt.

- ♪ ♪ ♪ -

Building a business was burdensome. I was passionate about my work, but the transition from our vacation back to reality was more difficult for us than we expected. We came back to problems. We had faced many obstacles during our twelve years in business—low cash flow, employee issues, disloyal clients and staff, and clients who made unreasonable demands and constantly quibbled over fees—but suddenly we were confronted with a situation that did irreparable damage to us both financially and emotionally. Our senior accountant and staff manager whom we trusted and had considered making a partner, conspired to steal our clients away as he was opening his own accounting firm. He had been with us for more than three years and had established good relationships and built up trust with a large portion of our restaurant clients.

As much as I loved ADL & Co., the overall management of the company was Arty's domain. He dealt with all the major obstacles on a daily basis. My job was the fun part, and I only had to face the tough stuff when Arty chose to share problems with me that held back our progress. This employee's deceit was a serious offense.

Arty's voice sounded like the roar of a jet engine when he told me and Gary what had happened. His fists were clenched, and his face was contorted. "Do you want to do the dirty work and throw him out or do you want me to do it?" he questioned Gary.

Gary was shocked. "I thought he was my close friend," Gary said as he smacked his fist against the wall. "We went to college together. How could he do this?" Gary paused. "Let's fire him together, let's do it now!" he said, storming around the office in a rage.

Arty calmed down as he swiveled in his chair. "We must be strategic. We can't afford to lose any business," he said as he pulled his chair up to his desk and began to make a list of the clients the manager handled. "Gary, you call this half and I'll call the rest. Let's meet later this afternoon and then we'll throw him out."

Fortunately we kept most of our clients, but had to quickly find someone else to replace the disloyal thief.

"I hate employees," Arty said as he began to write an ad for the *New York Times* help wanted section. "None of them are loyal, but this one was the worst."

I sat with Arty while he placed the ad. He looked up at me and said, "I don't know how much longer I can do this. I'm not getting any younger." He hesitated and stood up. "How do I know if the new person we hire will be trustworthy? I can't go through this again." He turned toward me, and took a deep breath. "I want to sell...I want out," he said.

I knew Arty was speaking from his heart, but I was torn. I loved this company that we had created. I enjoyed establishing new relationships, bringing in new business, and maintaining respect and a high profile in the business community. I was fortunate, because I didn't carry the burden of running the business like Arty did—I didn't have to worry about a lot of issues: employee concerns, paying the rent, the anxieties of the clients and their money, or the day to day minutia of growing. I listened intently to Arty's feelings, but I wanted to fight him.

In my soul, though, I knew Arty was right; I too was getting older. I admit it, I liked living the good life—the fancy vacations, dinners in the best restaurants, shopping at Bergdorf Goodman, buying gifts for my grandkids, and living in penthouse apartments. However, the bigger our business got, the bigger the problems became. I didn't want to sell, but if it was causing my beloved husband so much pain, was it worth keeping? Trying to remain calm, I rested my elbow on my thigh and put the upper side of my hand on my chin, as if I were Rodin's sculpture, *The Thinker*.

Arty knelt down beside me and spoke softly rubbing his hand on my leg. "The timing is right to sell our business, because accounting firms are consolidating—the Big Eight are now the Big Six and smaller accounting firms are merging with larger ones," he told me. "If we keep the business, we will start to have a hard time finding the right employees, since most will want to go to the Big Six and they pay better." Arty's pleading voice compelled me to listen. "I'm over sixty and I've been doing this work for more than thirty years. I'm tired. We've built a nice business together. Having the hospitality market as our niche makes us very desirable, and I think we can sell it for enough money to secure our retirement. Ever since we returned from Italy, I have the travel bug and I want to do more," he continued. "If we sell the business we can see the world before we're too old and have to use walkers to get around." He pointed to a travel guide of Sicily that he had sitting on his desk.

I sat in silence. Why should I fight him? I believed it was a battle I couldn't win, and in reality, I wasn't sure I wanted to. Arty was usually right about these kinds of decisions, and if we could sell for enough money, I thought it would make our life easier and take the burden off of him. I didn't want him to get sick, or worse, die.

I felt conflicted. "But what about Gary and Kenny? What will happen to them? What about me? Whom will you sell to? What if I don't like the buyers? What if I don't like working for anyone else?" I rambled in a panic.

Arty pulled me up from the chair and grabbed my arms. "What if are my two least favorite words," he said shaking his head. "Do you think I would put you at risk? I want to be safe, too. And don't worry about the boys. They're young." He released my arms. "I will interview many firms before I make a decision, and when I have an agreement I will negotiate jobs and a salary for the boys and of course for us too," he said confidently. "Don't have an anxiety attack. This is going to take a while. It will be a long process, but I need to start now."

I sat in disbelief. I repeated my mother's words over and over again—what will be, will be. The tension in my body slowly released.

Arty met with Gary and Ken to tell them about his plans. Gary agreed with Arty's decision, as long as the money was right and he had a secure position. Ken was confident that Arty would take care of him.

In September 1999, Arty began searching for the right firm to sell the business to. His first step was to call a business broker, and also spread the word in the industry. The potential buyer had to meet his criteria: the selling price, accountability, secure positions for Gary, Ken and me, and perhaps most importantly, the buyer needed to share a similar philosophy to ours on running a business that included client service and employee management. Arty interviewed more than a dozen accounting firms before he found the right one.

A year later, Arty began negotiating with his firm of choice—the largest public accounting firm in New Jersey. ADL & Co. would be their entrée into New York City. I remember Arty and Gary sitting around the conference table with the new buyers hashing out the financial settlement. Ken and I were not included in this meeting; since we weren't CPAs, we were not considered to be legal partners. I paced the hall nervously, waiting for the outcome. It seemed like hours before Arty emerged from the conference room. Then he buzzed his secretary and asked her to send me and Ken to the conference room.

"Welcome to ADL & Co. You are going to love it here," I told the new owners. "Our clients, the FBC, the networking...it's all great," I continued to ramble as I pointed to some of our framed articles hanging on the wall. We talked for a short while longer and then said our goodbyes.

"Have your due diligence team call me to set up an appointment," Arty said as he walked the principals of the company, two men in their early fifties, to the door. "As soon as the financials are cleared, we can finalize the agreement and the merger will be complete."

I sat in the conference room with Gary and waited for Arty to see them out. Ken went back to his office and Gary and I joked about having new bosses. We both looked up when Arty returned to discuss the logistics of the merger. "Whew," Arty said. "The pressure will finally be off, and it will be nice to receive a nice lump sum at first and then a check every month for the next ten years without having the grief of running the business." His smile lit up his face as he looked at us.

I was completely filled with happiness. But it was short lived.

"What's wrong," I said looking at Gary. He had stopped smiling and nervously picked at his fingernails.

"I don't know how to tell you this," he said as he cleared his throat, directing his remarks to Arty. "But, I don't feel like I'm getting a fair share of the money. I deserve more," Gary said as he sat up straight and placed his hands flat on the table. "I built this firm to what it is today; you couldn't have done it without me."

"What did you say?" Arty asked raising his voice.

"You're not giving me enough money. I want more." Gary answered as if he were giving his father an order.

I sat silently with my hands tightly clasped on the table. Arty's shoulders tensed up.

He then spoke assertively. "You're not entitled to more—your mother and I built this business from the ground up—it was twelve hard years of our blood and sweat," he said as he raised his voice even louder. "You've only been with us for five of those years."

Arty got up, and raised his arms in disgust. "No. No. No more money." He took a deep breath and said, "If I give you more, it comes out of my pocket. This is the retirement fund for me and your mother. We need every bit of it!"

It was like war of the worlds with Gary storming out of the room screaming, "Then we have no deal!"

It was one of the most painful fights I have ever observed between a father and his son. My body shook with pain. Arty and I didn't know what to do. The merger had to happen. I went to stand beside Arty and slowly rubbed his back.

"What will you do?" I asked, my eyes welling up with unshed tears.

"I don't know," he said. "I carved out enough money from the sale to provide Gary with a nice financial cushion. He has to take into consideration that he'll make a very substantial salary and as a senior partner reap the benefits of the profits annually." Arty continued to rationalize. "I've always said that when money rears its ugly head, life can get uglier."

We were in a state of shock. We felt paralyzed.

I phoned Dr. Watkins. Speaking to her, I cried so hard I could hardly catch my breath. We had only been seeing her intermittently by that point, but she said that if we needed to we could come in for a session. Her calming voice quieted me. "Let them work it out together, they always do," she said. Arty and I sat through dinner hardly talking. My eyes were swollen and red from crying and I watched as he poured himself a stiff drink.

"How could he do this to us?" Arty questioned as he sipped his martini. "I'm retiring." Taking another sip, he said, "I have no choice but to negotiate with him."

The due diligence team did their inspection, and everything was falling into place with the exception of Arty and Gary's split. Rather than trust his father, Gary met with an outside consultant, a retired CPA, who advised him in the financial negotiations, urging him to focus on his own self interests. To this day I still don't know why he met with someone who knew nothing about our business or our family.

"How could this guy know anything? He didn't work in our firm; he only knows what Gary tells him." Arty said angrily. "A mediator would be better, but I'll get it done...I'll get it done," he repeated. "Unfortunately, we have no choice."

Arty's and Gary's negotiations went on for almost a month. They had daily meetings about the buyout and sometimes there were even after hours phone calls. A few conversations were more heated than others and ended up with either Arty or Gary walking out. Finally, they came to an agreement: Gary would get more money, and Artys' retirement package would end at an earlier age. They had both compromised. I was only happy it was over and they were not enemies.

Finally, in February 1999, ADL & Co. merged with J. H. Cohn LLP, which at that time was the 25th largest accounting firm in the country. Arty, Gary and I went to Union Square Cafe to celebrate. I remember raising our glasses toasting to our success. I don't know why but just then Gary suddenly realized that Arty's share of the proceeds from the sale were only good until he turned seventy-two. Buttering a piece of bread, he sounded cavalier as he said, "It's not enough, you'll only be seventy-two years old when the money from the sale runs out." Arty nodded as he cut a piece of steak. He didn't want to go back, he didn't want the pain; it was enough and somehow he knew that we'd survive.

Perhaps Gary's acknowledgment of the short term payout and the money he demanded was his way of apologizing or perhaps he was acknowledging his guilt. I never knew the answer...and never asked him.

The merger went smoothly. Gary was secure in his position as a senior partner in charge of all of the restaurant clients, Ken and I ran the FBC, and Arty's contract stated that he would stay on for the next two to three years managing the family business practice and making sure the transition of clients went smoothly. I planned to retire with Arty, but my life continued to beat to the fast-paced drums of the kinetic Bolero dance, and it soon became clear that destiny had other plans for me.

- ♪ ♪ ♪ -

Argentine Tango

The dance called the Tango was brought to
Argentina by numerous European immigrant
channels, which included black slaves, and the
rhythm they were known for. Argentine Tango is
a sad, melancholy, dance. It includes all the traits
of society: frustration, unhappiness, rancor,
nostalgia, and resentment.

Cancer

The slow rhythmic pace of the Argentine Tango
played with our emotions and taught us the beat
of life's dance is within our hearts.
This was one dance we wouldn't sit out.

I returned from the July 4th holiday weekend at our vacation home in the Berkshires in good spirits. Gary was speaking with his secretary when I stopped by his office to say hello.

"How was your weekend? How's my precious Andrew? Is he walking yet?" I peppered him with questions. Andrew, my fifth grandchild, had turned one two weeks earlier.

"We had a great weekend; we took Andrew to the pool," Gary told me. I knew Andrew loved the water. Also with Gary and his family moving from their townhouse in Tarrytown, New York to a new house in Scarsdale, New York in a few weeks, they wanted their son to enjoy the pool as much as possible. "I'll tell you all about it later," he said. "I just want to finish up coordinating my schedule."

As I started to walk away, Gary called out to me.

"Mom, (Where's Ro—why is he calling me mom?), I was shaving this morning and found a lump in my neck. It doesn't hurt, but I still think I should make an appointment with the doctor just to have it checked out."

"Where is it?" I asked. Gary pointed to the lump just below his left earlobe. I ran my finger across it. "It's nothing to worry about," I said. "It's probably a swollen gland. I'm sure the doctor will just give you an antibiotic to prevent an infection."

- ♪ ♪ ♪ -

It was July 31, 2002. I had been studying Italian, and two of my friends and I met once a month for lunch to practice speaking the language with our Italian tutor. We always dined at an Italian restaurant to make us feel like we were in Italy for those few hours. Alfredo's Restaurant at Rockefeller Center, famous for their Fettuccine Alfredo, was this month's choice.

"Ciao," I said as I greeted the host. "Buon Giorno." Smiling, he took me to my table. I was the last to arrive. My friends were already engaged in conversation.

"Como siete?" I interrupted. "Parlate lentamente. Voglio a comprendere," I said as I sat down. They laughed. We ordered our lunch in Italian and continued the conversation.

"Scusi," the Maître d' interrupted. "Ms. Levy, you have a phone call."

I got up quickly and walked to the phone. Who would be calling me? Only Arty knew where I was.

"Hello?" Before I had a chance to say another word, Arty

said, "Ro, you need to come back to the office right away. There's something we need to talk about." He sounded concerned.

"Why do I have to come back?" I demanded. My mind began to race with worry. Arty wouldn't call and interrupt my lunch if there wasn't a problem. "Please tell me," I begged. "What's wrong?"

"It's Gary. He had a biopsy this morning." He hesitated as if he couldn't get the words out. Then he said it. "Gary has a malignancy; he has cancer."

I sat down heavily in a chair next to the phone. I couldn't believe his words. How could this be? Gary was fine. His color was good. He wasn't losing weight. I felt faint.

"Wait there and I'll pick you up," Arty said. "Gary is waiting for us at a restaurant near the hospital with Robyn and Andrew."

I remembered Gary telling me that he had a lump. This couldn't be true, I thought. It was only a swollen gland. I sat there in disbelief, waiting for Arty to pick me up from the restaurant.

In the taxi, Arty and I held hands and looked at each other—we were both in shock. We grew up in the '50s when the word "cancer" was a death sentence. This couldn't be happening, I rationalized. This only happens to other people. I started thinking the "what ifs." What if it spread? What if they can't cure him? What if he dies? I began to cry and Arty put his arms around me.

"Everything will be alright," I asked, "*Right*?" Arty had always tried to reassure me, only this time he had no answer.

We arrived at the restaurant. Gary's wife had tears in her eyes as she handed me the baby. Holding Andrew put a smile on my face, yet when I looked at Gary reality took over. He just stared straight ahead, nodding a brief hello to me, his brow furrowed. He looked fragile. I was scared.

Robyn took Gary for a C.A.T. scan that afternoon, while Arty and I took care of Andrew. We were anxious to hear the results: What type of cancer was it? Had it spread? And if so, where? It was difficult to focus, yet Andrew kept our minds occupied as he crawled throughout our apartment. The bathroom was his favorite room, and as he stood next to the toilet bowl trying to splash the water around, his innocence was refreshing. We laughed as we dragged him away and closed the door.

Two hours later Gary and Robyn arrived at our apartment. Robyn picked up Andrew and gave him a hug.

"Are you happy to see mommy?" Andrew giggled as he squirmed in her arms wanting to be put down. We noticed that she had been crying.

Gary sat on the couch. He looked disheveled and I imagined that his body had been poked and prodded for hours by doctors and radiologists. He fought back his tears and his voice quivered as he began to speak.

"I have a tumor on my tonsil," he said. "It's cancer of the tonsil. That's the bad news. The worse news is that it has spread to a lymph node" (I gasped, remembering the lump in his neck). "But there is some good news," he said. "It hasn't spread to my lungs or brain."

Gary hunched his shoulders; he slumped his head into his hands, and after a few moments, looked up. His dark brown eyes cried out, "mommy, make me better." I was in horrific emotional pain but managed to maintain my composure. I put my hand soothingly on his knee as Arty sat next to him. Robyn stood nearby crying softly. We sat in silence and watched

Andrew play with his toys.

- ♪ ♪ ♪ -

I awoke the next morning staring at the horizontal shades covering my bedroom window. They were sheer, yet filtered the light and gave me the privacy I wanted when the panes were closed. I thought I was dreaming as I saw the sunlight peek through. I rubbed my eyes as if to brush away the truth of Gary's cancer.

I looked at Arty. He was still asleep. My mind started to race. What do we do next? Where do we go from here? As I reached to wake Arty up, I remembered that we were supposed to leave for a week of golf camp in San Diego that afternoon. We had planned this vacation six months earlier.

"Arty, Arty...wake up...wake up. We're supposed to leave for San Diego this afternoon. Golf camp, remember?" Arty shifted, slowly blinking his eyes once or twice and sat up.

"What?"

"We're supposed to leave for golf camp today. What do we do?"

He looked at me and without hesitation said, "Cancel the trip."

I phoned Gary early that morning. The phone rang and rang and finally he answered it. His voice on the other end sounded abrupt and angry. He was entitled, I thought, he had cancer. Why did he get cancer? Where did it come from? Was it something in our genes? I questioned myself over and over.

"How are you feeling?" I asked compassionately.

"I'm OK. As well as can be expected, considering I have cancer." He paused, took a deep breath, and continued on, his voice slightly calmer. "I've been doing lots of research on the Internet looking for answers about cancer of the tonsil; the survivor stats, the treatment, the cure, and the doctors," he told me. "I need to have answers," he said emphatically.

I wanted to soothe him and give him answers, but no words came out.

"I have an appointment today with the Chief of Head and Neck Surgery at NYU Medical Center. My emotions are mixed. I don't know what to think, or who or what to believe. I am counting on the surgeon to make me better and get rid of my cancer, now!" he screamed into the phone.

We had known Gary to be a procrastinator, but in this case he was anxious to make a decision and wasn't thinking about repercussions. Now he knew he couldn't be wrong—it was a matter of life or death.

"Meet me and Robyn at the Medical Center at one o'clock; the doctor's office is on the sixth floor," he said and hung up.

It was blazing hot that day. I noticed the black tar oozing and was careful not to step on the softer spots as we crossed Second Avenue at 33rd Street heading for the Medical Center. My head felt heavy on my shoulders with the heat adding to the weight. Will we like the surgeon? Will he make Gary better? Again, the "what ifs" bombarded my mind. What if the surgeon can't make Gary better? What if we don't like the surgeon? What if? What if? As we entered the hospital, the burst of cool air from the air conditioned lobby felt refreshing. Following the sign, Head and Neck Surgery, we took the elevator and pressed the button for the sixth floor.

Gary, Robyn, and Andrew were already there when we arrived. Gary held Andrew on his lap. Robyn was leaning her head on Gary's shoulder. It would have been a nice family photo had we not been sitting in the waiting room in a hospital. Andrew's nanny sat across from Robyn and Gary and entertained Andrew by making silly faces.

The waiting room was a typical one with magazines strewn about on the end tables showing the wear and tear of patients flicking through. There were six other patients in the room—a mix of young and old. I glanced at them, wondering if they had cancer too.

As I waited for the doctor to see us, I felt beads of sweat build up and trickle down my back. My palms were clammy. Blotting my forehead, I wondered if Gary was as anxious as I was. Was he sweating? Was his stomach in knots? I could only imagine. What was Robyn thinking? What about Arty?

The nurse broke through my thoughts when she presented Gary with the insurance and medical history forms for him to fill out. Shortly after she called out his name.

"Gary Levy." We all stood up. "Please follow me." Robyn handed Andrew to his nanny.

As we entered the examining room, I took note of the chair, which resembled a dentist's chair, and glanced at the wall which was lined with diplomas and other certificates affirming the doctor's credentials.

"Sit here," the nurse said, "The doctor will be with you in a moment."

Gary sat down. Resisting sitting back, he sat on the edge firmly gripping the arms of the chair. Tapping his right foot as if he had a nervous twitch, he appeared to be taking his own visual notes. There was a computer directly behind the chair with an overhead light above that illuminated the examination area. Other instruments on a rolling cart looked like tools they used in the movie *Young Frankenstein*. Shivering momentarily, I thought, well, at least he isn't having a lobotomy.

"Good afternoon, I'm Dr. Delacure," the doctor said as he entered the room. He was a tall man with broad shoulders, strawberry blond hair, deep blue eyes, and a freckled face. His friendly smile and self assured manner made me feel confident. Gary shook his hand and filled the doctor in on the events of the last twenty-four hours. After listening to the data, the doctor proceeded to examine Gary.

"Sit back and open your mouth wide. This might be a bit uncomfortable but it won't hurt," he said.

He turned on the overhead light, and after spraying Gary's throat with a numbing substance, the doctor took a long thin plastic tube off of the rolling cart and slid it gently down Gary's throat. The computer screen displayed its path—and then we saw the tumor—it was big and black. I cringed and grabbed Arty's hand tightly. I squinted, not wanting to see the truth.

Turning off the light, Dr. Delacure confirmed the diagnosis, cancer of the tonsil, and said it was Stage 4 cancer.

"Stage 4? What does that mean?" I asked anxiously.

"It's when the cancer metastasizes and spreads. In this case it has spread to the lymph nodes in his neck. We can't be sure how many nodes it has spread to, but we will treat Gary aggressively since he's young and in good shape," Dr. Delacure said confidently. "I will be the surgeon overseeing his case, and I believe that the combination of chemotherapy, radiation, and surgery should kill the cancer."

I clung to every word as if I were listening to God.

Trying to lighten the seriousness of the situation, the doctor added, "You can even decide to have a nose job or an eye lift during the surgery and get a whole new look from the neck up."

Gary tried to smile and said, "Just get rid of the cancer."

I watched Gary's body language. He was sitting up taller, had released his tight grip on the arms of the chair, and seemed more relaxed. He appeared to have bonded with the doctor and to trust him.

Doctor Delacure gave Gary his recommendation for a radiation oncologist but also suggested that Gary interview a few other radiation oncologists before he made his final choice. Gary agreed. They shook hands, and Gary made an appointment with him for the following week.

As fate would have it, Gary and Robyn's scheduled moving date was the same day as his appointment with Doctor Delacure's recommended radiation oncologist. Meeting with this doctor was a priority, so Arty and I took on the job of working with the moving men.

We arrived at Gary's house to find the living room filled with wall-to-wall cartons and furniture wrapped in quilted blankets sealed with heavy duty duct tape. Andrew crawled between the boxes and gave us a big smile. He reached his arms to be picked up. I gave him a big hug as Robyn and Gary gave us instructions for the movers. I had no time for tears.

"We should be back home at about one o'clock; we'll meet you at our new home. Hopefully you'll have us all moved in," Gary said glibly.

I watched them drive away and hoped that this doctor would be the answer to our prayers. Tuning away from the window, I went to pack up the last few boxes.

Gary and Robyn arrived at their new home late in the afternoon. Arty was directing the movers and I was unpacking kitchenware. We stopped immediately when we saw Gary. He looked weary and Robyn was acting stoic. Rather than enjoying the excitement of their new home, they were preoccupied with their day's events. Their appearance made me uneasy—did we need to get prepared to hear more bad news?

"Come over here and sit down. There are only a few more cartons to empty and then the kitchen will be in order. I can make some tea, do you want a cup?" I asked. "Did you like the doctor? Was his diagnosis the same?" I rambled out of nervousness. Gary held his head in his hands. Robyn massaged his back as he began to speak in nearly a whisper.

"I don't doubt the credentials of the doctors at Sloan Kettering and NYU Medical Center, but I've made my decision. I'm going to go with Dr. Louis Harrison, the head of radiation oncology at Beth Israel Medical Center," he told us.

"I picked him not only for his excellent credentials, but I also like his bedside manner and I am confident he will stay by my side at all times. And Robyn liked him, too. I have an appointment with him next week to schedule six weeks of radiation treatments and to measure my face for a mesh screen to protect it from the radiation."

Arty and I were glad he had made a decision. The waiting was over and Gary's road to wellness would soon begin. Thank you God, I mumbled under my breath.

Arty and I returned home that evening, consumed by mental and physical exhaustion. The concierge greeted us. "Ms. Levy, we have a delivery for you," he said and handed me a beautiful orchid plant. Who would send me a plant and why? I wondered. The card that came with the plant read: all of our love and good wishes for Gary's speedy recovery. "It's from Karen and Mickey Peterson," I told Arty. "Why did they have to send a plant? A card or a phone call would have been enough."

As we entered the apartment, I set the plant on the kitchen counter. Taking off my shoes, I sat on the couch and stared at the plant. What did this plant symbolize? I don't want to care for a plant. What if it dies? Would that mean Gary would die if I couldn't take care of it, or if I couldn't take care of him? I shook my head to rid it of my negative thoughts. The phone rang. It was my niece, Eve, my sister's daughter.

"Hi, Auntie Ro. How are you and Uncle Arty? How's Gary doing? We are thinking of you."

"We're hanging in there," I replied.

I love my niece, and briefly filled her in on the events of the day. But at that moment I only focused on the plant. All of a sudden looking at the orchid, I started to cry.

"What's wrong?" she asked.

I could barely catch my breath. "It's the plant...A friend sent us a plant," I said through sobs. "I can't care for this plant. I don't want it." I cried harder. "I must get rid of it now! I'll call you back."

Hanging up, as tears rolled down my cheeks, I yelled out to Arty who had escaped to the bedroom to remove himself from the day's activities. "I can't keep this plant—it's a symbol of something, I don't know what, but I must give it away, I can't take care of it. I'm going to the lobby. I'll give it to the handyman, the concierge, the doorman, I don't care who takes it. I just can't keep it!" Arty nodded as if he understood.

I stood in the lobby barefoot on the cool marble tiles. I was still sobbing. Handing the orchid plant to the concierge, I pleaded with him to do away with it; to keep it or give it to someone else. "I don't care what you do with it, don't tell me, please. Please just get rid of it," I cried. Without asking any questions, he took the plant and told me not to worry. Thanking him, I felt relieved and returned back to the apartment.

The next day we drove to Gary and Robyn's new house to help them get settled in, and unpack more boxes. Gary met us at the door and before I had a chance to enter, he handed me a book, entitled, *It's Not About the Bike*, by Lance Armstrong.

"It's about Lance's battle with cancer," he said. "He writes that cancer is the best thing that happened to him." Then, with a sweet look on his face, Gary read me a piece from the book. "His story is helping me deal with my cancer. I'm connecting with him.

It gives me a greater understanding of the toll cancer takes and its effects, not only on me, but also on my family and friends. You *must* read it."

I looked at the cover and read the blurbs on the back. I latched onto anything that would help me know what Gary had to go through. Lance had only been given a 20% chance of surviving and Gary had a better than 85% chance. The odds were in our favor and if Lance Armstrong could come back from his deathbed to win another Tour de France, Gary could certainly use him as a role model to win his own battle. *It's Not About The Bike* became my newest Bible.

- ♪ ♪ ♪ -

On August 9, 2002, Gary was admitted to the ninth floor, the floor for all cancer patients at Beth Israel Medical Center. He would be there two nights. As we got off the elevator I observed the cancer patients—some of them walked the floor pushing their IV drip; some sat in wheelchairs as if they were looking to be entertained—and others just lay around in their beds, just waiting, waiting...I hoped not waiting to die.

When we arrived, Robyn was sitting alone in Gary's room. He was in surgery to have a peg for a feeding tube implanted in his stomach. The intensity of the radiation treatments would burn his throat and the peg was a precautionary measure.

Coming out from the surgery, Gary was groggy. His words were garbled as he tried to speak.

"I feeeee...l as if I was punch...ed in the stomach—it reall...

y hurr...hurtsssss," he cried pointing to his incision from the operation.

"Just rest," I said. He closed his eyes.

A few minutes later he awoke. His words still slurred, he said, "I have to pe-e-e."

Leaning on Arty, Gary's legs gave way. I watched in fear—what was happening to my son? I panicked and called for the nurse. Rushing into his room, the nurse said,

"You must stay in bed; I'll get you the urine bottle."

Shaking his head no in defiance, Gary grabbed onto Arty's arm. The nurse, who was unwilling to fight with him, took Gary's other arm and between the two of them they slowly walked Gary to the bathroom. Once he was back in bed, Gary looked relieved. Eventually, the drug began to wear off and was able to speak more clearly.

Arty and I stayed with Gary until he was more comfortable. It was hard to leave him, since he'd never been in a hospital before. Wanting to make him feel better, I fluffed the flat hospital pillows, smoothed out the sheets, and made sure he drank fluids, because the doctors told us his fluid intake was important. Robyn had left the hospital a bit earlier to be home with Andrew before he went to bed. When Gary had trouble keeping his eyes open, we kissed him on his forehead and said good night.

We arrived at the hospital early the next morning. To my surprise Gary was sitting up in bed eating breakfast. Seeing him in good spirits made me happy.

"What's for breakfast?" I asked.

"Scrambled eggs with bacon, toast, orange juice, and coffee."

he told us. "And it's not bad for hospital food. I guess I'm hungry."

Considering that he was scheduled to undergo his first chemo cycle and radiation treatment that day, Gary was calm.

"How was your night?" I asked.

"The bed is very uncomfortable, the pillows suck, and the sheets feel like sandpaper. My belly was sore from the peg so I had the nurse give me a painkiller which knocked me out. Only one more night of this...later on, Robyn is bringing me my pillow. I want to get started with the treatments already and go home," he said.

Robyn arrived, Gary's pillow in hand, at the same time that the nurse came in with the first chemo bag. The bag of clear liquid was marked with a big black X and the word POISON glared.

Gary got up and sat in a wheelchair, grimacing as the nurse gently punctured his arm with the IV needle. She worked quickly and efficiently, as she tapped the chemo bag slightly, to be sure the flow of the clear liquid could freely pass through the thin tube. Her precise execution demonstrated her compassion for her patients.

"I'm done, Gary. You have two bags of chemo that will take five hours to go through your body. You won't be in any pain, but we will watch you closely for any reaction," the nurse told him. "After lunch, we will take you for your first radiation treatment, and tomorrow you can go home." Patting him on his shoulder, she walked away.

"Thanks," Gary responded as she left his room. Turning to us he said, "Let's hang out in the lounge. We can play Scrabble."

It was as if he was oblivious to the poison entering his body. I wondered if his nonchalant pretense was covering up his fear.

Robyn wheeled Gary to the lounge as Arty pushed the IV stand. Anxiously, I watched, cringing as the chemo dripped slowly into my son's body. Playing Scrabble took us away from reality. Each of us tried to outdo the other with words we had never heard of. Gary won and I wanted to believe this was significant somehow. I was willing to grab on to any straw.

After lunch the nurse came to take Gary down for his radiation treatment. We followed as she wheeled him around with the chemo IV still attached. While Gary waited his turn, Dr. Harrison met with us. A man in his late forties, he had a small narrow frame. His brown hair was thinning and his green eyes radiated a demure, mild manner, yet he was serious, soft spoken, and confident. I immediately felt calmer in his presence.

Dr. Harrison spent ten minutes explaining the procedure to us. He then transferred Gary to a stretcher and wheeled him into the room where he would have his first radiation treatment. Gary wore a hospital gown with the strings tied loosely showing some bare skin. The nurse covered him with a blanket, telling him the room was cold. I turned my head, unable to watch them wheel him away. Tears filled my eyes as I sat in the waiting room. Robyn looked at us, and said, "First my mother, now my husband. I can't bear it."

"How do you think I feel?" Arty responded. "First my mother has cancer, and now my son."

I wept in Arty's arms.

That night I stayed until visiting hours were over. I couldn't leave Gary knowing he had had both the radiation and chemotherapy treatments on the same day. After Arty and Robyn left, I didn't want

Gary to be alone so I bought him a brown teddy bear as tall as I was with a big red bow tied around his neck. I love the color red; my mother had often told me that it keeps the evil spirits away. At about 8:oo p.m., the floor was quiet. I sat next to the window; the big brown teddy placed in the chair next to me. Gary and I then spoke about his going home the next day.

"I can't wait to get out of here," he said. "I can't wait to see Andrew." Before he had a chance to say another word, the largest cockroach I had ever seen fell from the curtain onto my lap. I shrieked, "Oh my God, oh my God," and jumped up trying to brush what looked like an alien off of me. I grabbed the teddy and ran into the hall, without giving a thought to Gary.

"Nurse, nurse," I yelled. "Hurry, hurry...there's this giant bug, I think it's a bug and I'm scared!"

A male nurse came quickly holding his finger to his mouth as if to tell me to quiet down and followed me to Gary's room. Gary sat up in bed laughing.

"Where is it?" the nurse asked. "I'm not too fond of cockroaches either; I'll go get a broom."

Gary pointed to behind the door and said he saw the cockroach go in that general direction. I stood in the doorway peeking in and waited until the nurse came back.

"There it is, there it is," I yelled to the nurse as he returned with a broom. "It's crawling along the wall in the hall."

"Quick, quick hit it!"

Raising the broom above his head, the nurse swatted the giant roach mashing it into the floor as if it were a marshmallow. It was sad to watch him kill a living creature, but I hated roaches.

"There, it's done with. I'll get the janitor to clean it up."

I breathed a sigh of relief. "Thanks so much," I said and went back to be with Gary.

"Mom, you left me alone in here with that creature, how could you do that? It's a good thing I'm not afraid of bugs," Gary said with a laugh.

I was mortified. How could I do this? How could I have abandoned my son, especially now?

"I couldn't help myself. I'm sorry," I said filled with remorse. "I'm going home now. Teddy will keep you company. I love you. See you tomorrow." Kissing him on his cheek, I left. I was ridden with guilt. Past insecurities welled up; the old voices told me I wasn't good enough, wasn't worthy. I doubted my ability to be strong.

- ♪ ♪ ♪ -

Gary's first day home from the hospital was difficult. He was weak and nauseous from the chemotherapy. I brought him chicken soup thinking it would make him feel better, but he took one look at the soup and ran to the bathroom to vomit. Later that day Robyn and I forced Gary to join us and Andrew at their neighborhood playground.

"It will do you good to be out of bed and get some fresh air," Robyn said.

He resisted. I helped her pull him from the bed. He was too weak to fight. It was a beautiful summer day; the blue sky had wisps of clouds, there was a cool breeze and the scent of daisies from the neighboring yards tickled our noses. Slowly we walked to the playground. Gary sat on the bench while Robyn pushed Andrew on the swing. I sat with Gary. Thank goodness I didn't see any bugs.

Arriving back at the house, I told Gary he had to eat.

"No, I don't want anything. I'm going back to bed," he said.

I followed him upstairs begging him. "I'll make you red Jell-o, you love red Jell-o, or vanilla pudding your favorite. Please Gary, please eat something."

Knowing how important it was for him to eat, I made the Jell-o and vanilla pudding. I brought it upstairs and gave him a choice. He turned away from me. I pleaded with him, and proceeded to spoon feed him, first the pudding, then the Jell-o. He ate a little and then pushed my hand away. I covered him, and left the room. Wiping away my tears with my shirtsleeve, I walked downstairs.

"I'm going home," I told Robyn. Kissing her and Andrew, I said, "See you tomorrow. Call me if you need me."

Gary's radiation treatment went on for five days a week for six weeks, and twice a day for the last two weeks. The radiation was so intense his neck turned a bright red as if he were badly burned. The reports from the doctors were good. The tumor was shrinking faster than they anticipated and his prognosis was getting better every day. But before the cancer would be gone, Gary had to endure yet another cycle of chemotherapy. After the third week of radiation, his throat was so sore that he had to go to peg feeding. He'd secure a tube to the peg implanted in his stomach and use an attached bag hooked to an IV pole to hold the liquid diet, Ensure, allowing it to drip slowly into the tube. He constantly spit mucous and kept boxes of tissues and waste paper baskets next to his bed. I had great difficulty watching him, but stood consistently by his side—with the exception of the roach.

After two months Gary's radiation and chemotherapy was finished. His tumor had shrunk completely and we were optimistic that he had gotten rid of the cancer for good. He had one month to heal and then would have surgery to remove the lymph node, as a precautionary measure.

On November 1, 2002, Gary was admitted to NYU Medical Center where Dr. Delacure performed neck surgery. Gary appeared totally healthy as he walked with Dr. Delacure to the operating room. As I watched from behind, I saw the doctor put his arm around Gary's shoulder. Even though they looked like long lost pals it pained me to watch. Did they really have to operate on Gary? Intellectually I understood, but emotionally I had a hard time with it.

The surgery lasted four hours and was successful. They found some traces of cancer cells but they were all dead, killed by the chemo and radiation. We were overwhelmed with happiness. Gary was cancer free and a cancer survivor. This time, the tears I cried were tears of joy. Our brutal Tango dance of continuous visits to hospitals and Gary's countless surgeries and chemo and radiation treatments was finally over.

- ♪ ♪ ♪ -

Salsa

*The Mambo dance in the 1950s was significant
because it would eventually morph into
the dance known as the Salsa. It is not known
whether this dance began in Cuba or Puerto Rico,
but Cuba's influence in North America
was weakened after Castro's revolution.
Salsa is one of the main dances in Cuba and
Puerto Rico today and it is danced all over the world.*

Hot Sexy Salsa

**A few dance lessons,
an exciting trip and Salsa
redefines our retirement.**

Arty's intention was to retire a year earlier, but he agreed to stay on and take care of Gary's clients while Gary was in cancer treatment. Meanwhile, I stopped working the moment I found out Gary had cancer. My job as his mother was my priority. Ken took over for me and managed the FBC.

Once Gary was in recovery, I felt free for the first time in a very long time, but Arty still had to fulfill the terms of his contract.

"If it wasn't for Gary, I'd leave tomorrow," Arty told me as he got dressed to go to the office. "Other than to take care of Gary's clients, I have no reason to go in. I have no motivation, I'm not appreciated, and I'm bored."

"Hang in there. Gary will be back at work right after the first of January. It's only a couple of months, and besides we have golf camp booked right after Gary returns," I said, straightening his tie.

Kissing me goodbye, he grabbed my hand. "I can't wait. I get up, go to work, come home, and go to bed. I'm miserable."

After he left, I started to think about how we'd fill our days after retirement. Our whole lives had revolved around raising our kids and building our business. Now, the kids were grown and the business was gone. We had never actually planned for retirement. I had just finished the most difficult job in my life which was taking care of Gary. I never thought I'd want to retire, but now I was really looking forward to it.

I picked up the phone and called a friend who had been a member of the women's forum I ran in the FBC.

"Want to meet me for lunch this afternoon?" I asked as I cleared off the breakfast table.

"I'd love to," she said. "Let's meet at the coffee shop at one."

All of my close friends from the FBC were peers. Most of us had either sold our businesses and retired or were currently in negotiation to do just that. Our conversation during lunch revolved around issues of retirement, menopause, and how to fill our days now that we no longer had a business.

"Let's start our own women's forum. I can ask Dr. Watkins to facilitate, you met her at one of our FBC meetings. She can help us decide what we want to do when we grow up!" I giggled as if I was a little girl and took a bite of my sandwich.

"What a good idea. It'll be a support group for the "golden girls," my friend said and laughed aloud.

We held the first session for the "golden girls" support group one month later. As I entered Dr. Watkins office, I reflected back to

Since I'm not good enough & project to everything else — it's not good enough the sessions that we had had with Arty and Gary—only now there were six chairs grouped around the glass top coffee table—and Dr. Watkins was the one sitting in the high-backed leather chair.

"Hi everyone," I said as I took my seat.

Dr. Watkins opened the session. "What are your objectives; what are your goals?" she asked as she picked up her yellow legal pad and pen. She looked at me. "Rosann, let's start with you."

It was a few moments before I answered, but I answered with certainty. "I want to be the master of my own destiny. I want to learn to enjoy life's changes and live my life to the fullest."

"Okay, that's great. Now, let's go around the room," said Dr. Watkins.

Learning how to make smooth transitions from the safe haven of the family business to the uncertainties of retired life was the theme of our first session. Dr. Watkins ended the session by teaching us five minutes of meditation. She explained that meditation would help us to find an inner peace and balance.

"Get in a comfortable position, feet flat on the floor, and close your eyes," she said. "Let the thoughts flow in and out and ground yourself by going back to your breath. Explore your body and breathe into any area in which you experience tightness or pain," she continued, as we all closed our eyes. Idle chatter filtered in and out of my brain as she spoke. What is Arty doing? Was he happy? I went back to my breath. More thoughts flowed in and out about Gary, my daughter, Tracy, who had just gotten divorced, and what I was going to do with the rest of my life? As I went back to my breath, I heard Dr. Watkins quietly ring a bell.

"Move your fingers, wiggle your toes, and open your eyes

slowly," she directed. I blinked and looked around the room at my friends, some of who had not yet opened their eyes. I felt at peace; my body was relaxed and my hands were limp in my lap. This was the fastest five minutes, I thought, as I sat quietly. Dr. Watkins broke the silence. "See you next month."

"Arty, Arty," I called excitedly as he walked through the door to our apartment after a day at work. "I had the best day. My women's group was great."

"Tell me about it later. I'm not interested right now." He walked into the kitchen and poured himself a drink.

I didn't pay attention to his demeanor. Excited to tell him about my experience, I pulled at his jacket sleeve and in a high pitched voice said, "I learned how to meditate this morning. Dr. Watkins told us meditating is like vacuuming your brain. I felt so calm, I almost fell asleep. Are you listening?" I tugged at him.

I felt like I was talking to myself, but I was too excited to stop. "Dr. Watkins conducts a mindfulness meditation workshop for six weeks and I signed up. Want to take it with me? You won't have to miss work, she holds them on weekends."

Shaking his head, he took a sip of his drink and plopped himself onto the couch. Finally, realizing that he was not in a good mood, I sat down next to him. "What's wrong?"

"I'm bored. I can't stand going to work. I feel like a robot," he said handing me the remote control. "Here, push the buttons and watch me move and make sounds like R2D2." My eyes opened wide as I watched him squeak and move mechanically. This can't be Arty, I thought. The alcohol must have gone to his head.

Trying to change his frame of mind, I stroked his thigh.

"Think happy thoughts; think about your retirement. You won't be accountable to anyone, and you'll be able to do anything you want."

"I can't let go," he said and wrinkled his brow.

Jumping up, I said, "I have an idea. We'll make a plan for your retirement now. Tell me the things you'd like to do and I'll write them down."

Arty smiled. "I like that idea. Let's make a list and tape it to the refrigerator. I want to look at it every day."

We spent the next hour making a list of our favorite activities; weekend getaways, hiking and biking trips, cooking classes, subscriptions to the theater, and at least one, if not two, big vacations a year. "I want to go back to Italy," he said as we lay in bed cuddling later that night. I felt close to him and kissed him on the cheek.

Our daily routines continued. Arty went to work. I made dates with friends, took yoga classes, and looked forward to my women's group with Dr. Watkins. I learned to do walking meditations and every breath I took was in sync with my stride. I followed the same path daily in Riverside Park along the Hudson River. I loved the feel of the wind blowing in my face and the smell of the sea water. I'd stop along the way and look at the ducks swimming, thinking how beautiful nature is. Occasionally I'd think of Arty. Was he doing OK? Was he still unhappy? I continued at my usual pace and by the end of my walks my head was distinctly clear. The leaves on the trees were greener, the sky appeared bluer, and the clouds looked like large puffs of cotton. I was at peace.

My daughter had introduced me to yoga, a Hindu discipline that unites the mind with the body As with meditation, my yoga practice gave me a quality of lucidity. Tracy had opened a studio in Connecticut, and I had a fantasy of possibly becoming a yoga teacher for children. I enrolled in a weekend workshop program and got my certification. I never got to teach children, but hung my certificate on my wall acknowledging yet another one of my accomplishments. Little did I know that Tracy's yoga studio would become a big part of my life later on in my retirement.

- ♪ ♪ ♪ -

Arty posted a calendar next to our plan and counted the days until his retirement. He seemed happier. We dined out two or three times a week and made sure to see all the new movies. I'd tell him about my daily experiences; sometimes he'd listen, other times he'd lose himself in watching sports. Unlike me, he had no interest in meditation or yoga.

In January 2003, Gary went back to work part time. Arty retired the following spring. Watching Arty pack his office was bittersweet. Helping him clear his bookshelves, I wiped a small layer of dust from the framed articles about ADL & Co and carefully placed them in cartons. Each one acknowledged his importance and affirmed his success in the business community. I was teary eyed, but looked forward to what the future would bring.

"Why are you saving that one?" he asked as he emptied his desk drawers. "It's a caricature from one of the Chamber events. It's not important."

"Everything is meaningful and I'm saving all of them," I said emphatically as I continued to remove smudges from the glass.

Arty reached for his favorite piece of memorabilia hanging on the wall opposite his desk. It was an authentic NFL jersey worn by Lawrence Taylor in the Super Bowl and autographed by the entire team. It was his prized possession and he held the oversized frame in his hands and hugged it to his chest.

"C'mon, put it on the dolly. Let's get out of here now," I said as I stood in the doorway. "I'm hungry, but we need to say our goodbyes before we can leave."

Arty took one last look around his office and we left. Tears rolled down my cheeks as we walked down the hall.

Following our plan, I booked our first getaway on Memorial Day Weekend 2003, thus kicking off our retirement. We stayed at an inn in Squam Lake, in New Hampshire. Ironically it was where the movie *On Golden Pond* had been filmed. What better place to begin our golden years? I thought. That weekend we biked, hiked, and rented a small powerboat to take in the sights of this scenic vacation spot.

"Arty, this is what life is all about. Retirement is going to be great. Look at the mountains surrounding us; the water is crystal clear and it's so peaceful," I said as I lay back on the boat, closing my eyes and letting the sun warm my face. "Let's stop at a beach for a swim."

Arty's face lit up with a big smile. I imagined piloting the boat safely around the lake gave him a sense of power. "I love this. Do you think we'll see Jane Fonda?" he said laughing as he pointed to the house where the movie had been shot.

Back in New York City, we enjoyed an active lifestyle. When we weren't working out at the gym, we took long walks in Riverside

Park, played golf at local public courses, and continued our bike rides around Manhattan or across the George Washington Bridge to New Jersey. We enrolled in a cooking class and learned how to prepare low calorie Italian dishes. I was empowered and believed Arty felt the same.

As the summer came to an end, though, Arty's mood changed. His appetite decreased and at most meals all he'd do is push around the food on his plate. He started waking up in the middle of the night and popped Tylenol PM so that he could sleep. I'd come home from yoga class and find him sitting on the couch channel surfing. "Don't you have anything better to do?" I asked as I placed my mat in the closet. "Why don't you come to yoga with me? It will get your blood circulating and give you energy." I was annoyed. How could he sit there day in and day out staring at the TV? I hoped this phase of his was just temporary. I couldn't understand why he was unhappy so at first I let his behavior slide. I mediated, spoke with my friends, and sometimes took two yoga classes a day looking for answers. This pattern continued for a couple of weeks, until I couldn't tolerate it anymore. I had to take control.

"Let's ride the loop in Central Park today," I yelled to Arty as I took my biking pants out of the drawer. "It's a beautiful fall day and the leaves are just beginning to change."

I walked into the living room. As usual, Arty was sitting on the couch channel surfing. If he wasn't watching TV—the Mets, or the Giants training for the upcoming season—he'd escape by reading some of the books on the *New York Times* best sellers list.

"Let's go on a bike ride," I repeated, trying to pull him off the couch.

"Leave me alone, I don't want to take a bike ride, we rode yesterday," he said and went back to channel surfing.

"Arty, I can't let you sit here and wither away," I said as I sat next to him.

"Retirement is not what it's made out to be." He looked at me and then turned back to the TV.

"When retirees have nothing to do, they die. I'm not going to let you die!" I said emphatically as I took his hand in mine.

"I have no purpose," he said pushing me away. "Stop nagging."

My emotions shifted from compassion to frustration. Why did he have a more difficult time than I did? I found things to do, things that made me happy. Perhaps this was a gender issue.

I walked back to the bedroom. "I'm going on a bike ride with or without you," I yelled as I put on my pants and tightened the Velcro band of my bike shoes.

Suddenly I was enraged, and confronted Arty as if I were a snorting bull about to attack the matador. "I've had it," I said as I went back to the living room. "You want to continue like this, then you're going to do it without me."

I raised my hands and in a firm voice said, "I will *not* live like this. I'll commit you to a psych ward first. You want to kill yourself, do it without me!" I paced the floor. "Your mind is the enemy of your body and you're letting it control your pain. You are not deathly ill."

I took a deep breath and changed my tone. "You'll survive. You must help yourself, but you're not even trying." I sat down on the ottoman in front of him. Arty finally stopped channel surfing.

· Cowering, he pleaded with me in a soft voice, "Don't yell at me, don't yell."

Had I finally gotten to him? Was he finally hearing me?

"If you can't get your shit together, then seek outside help or call Dr. Watkins."

He cleared his throat "OK, OK, I hear you," Arty put the remote on the couch. Thank God, I thought. I put my hands to my heart center as if I were in a yoga class about to *Om* and bowed my head.

"Let's take a short ride through Riverside Park and stop for a bite at the boat basin," I said, and I went to get him his biking attire.

As we were about to leave, the phone rang. It was my sister. For many years, our age difference kept us apart, but we were never estranged. Our instilled family values brought us closer together as we matured, and today we enjoy a great relationship which I cherish. But I am saddened by the fact that I have no relationship with my brother. At my father's funeral, he called himself "the black sheep of the family." He chose not conform with the accepted rules of society and opted for a life away from my sister, me, and our families.

"Hi Irm. How was your trip? Did you love Cuba?" I asked, sitting down on my bed.

"It was fabulous. Cuba is a beautiful country; you and Arty should definitely go for a visit," she said enthusiastically. "I'll send you photos."

Cuba would be a perfect vacation spot for us, since we already had a trip planned to Jamaica with our kids for the upcoming Christmas holiday. Because Cuba was difficult to get to from the United States, we could travel to Cuba from Jamaica, I figured.

That's it, I thought, a trip to Cuba. That would get Arty out of his slump; he would relish an exciting escapade that involved uncertainty and some risk.

"Arty, Arty," my voice went up an octave. "I just spoke to my sister. She loved Cuba and said that we absolutely have to go." I was so excited; I could barely catch my breath. "We can travel there from Montego Bay and after the kids leave we can spend a week in Havana."

"Cuba. Are you crazy? It's illegal," he said. "We can't use our credit cards, and if anything were to happen, we'd be in trouble." Picking up the remote control, he went back to watching the Mets.

"But my sister just came back from a vacation there, and she had no problems. We're going," I said adamantly. I was sure Cuba was the cure all for what ailed Arty.

I spent a week researching websites until I found a tour company that I believed was trustworthy. They arranged a tour guide and an itinerary that encompassed the main sights in Havana, including a day trip to the countryside.

The excitement of this adventure was infectious and our good friends, Mike, Marilyn, Steve, and Barbara decided to join us. Sharing this exotic journey with them added to my enthusiasm.

"We're booked," I said to Arty as I read the brochure and itinerary the tour company had sent me. I studied it closely and highlighted specific sights. As I continued reading, the words LEARN TO DANCE SALSA bounced off the page. I read it again. "Learn to dance salsa to the music of Celia Cruz," it said, "one of the most successful Cuban performers and internationally renowned as the Queen of Salsa."

Almost hyperventilating with excitement, I quickly got up off my chair. "Arty, we must learn to dance Salsa. Stop watching TV for a minute and look at me...*Look at me!* We must take dance lessons if we're going to go to Cuba. Salsa is the heart and soul of this country." I said pointing to the pamphlet.

Arty was vehement in his response. "*No.* No way. I have two left feet and no rhythm. I'll look like a fool. No. No. No...you'll never get me on a dance floor."

Using my feminine charm, I caressed his thighs, then his arms. "I'll make you a deal. I promise if you don't like it or have trouble learning we won't continue." I continued to coax him, looked at him coyly and passed my thumb over his lips. "Please, please," I pleaded, awaiting his response. He finally nodded OK. I jumped on his lap and hugged him.

We booked our introductory lesson in New York for the following week. Checking in at the front desk, I told the receptionist we were going to Cuba in December and wanted to learn Cuban Salsa. Before the gentleman had a chance to say anything, we heard a voice from behind us say, "I'm the King of Salsa, and I can teach you Cuban Salsa." I turned quickly and saw a tall lanky man with big black eyes, and dark curly hair raise his hand high above the line of people waiting to check in. I walked toward him and without hesitation I said, "If you're the King of Salsa, then you're it!"

His name was Eduardo Gonzalez and he had sex appeal. I noticed a rhythm in his stride as we followed him to a room in the back of the studio for our first lesson. We made our way through two separate ballrooms where a number of other couples were taking their lessons. "What dances are they doing?" I whispered to

Eduardo.

"A variety of dances: Fox Trot, Tango, Cha Cha, and Merengue," he said as he pointed to each of them. The beat of the music intrigued me. The adrenaline rushing through my body caused me to feel like butterflies were tickling my stomach, almost as if I were starting a new love relationship. I swayed my hips in sync to the Latin rhythms as we entered the room where we'd begin our lesson. It was small, with one wall covered with mirrors and tables and chairs lined up against the other.

Eduardo flicked through a folder of CDs and picked music recorded by the famed Cuban band, the Buena Vista Social Club. Looking at us he asked, "Are you ready for the Cuban Salsa?"

"Yes," we said in unison.

"Then place your right hand on your wife's back just below her shoulder blades and use a little pressure to direct her," Eduardo said to Arty, coordinating our stance. "Take her in your arms and place her right hand in your left. Maintain this posture as it teaches you the proper dance position."

Arty followed Eduardo's instruction and took me in his arms.

"Arty, now step forward on your right foot," Eduardo said and counted one. "Good, let's try that again. One, and again," he said as he counted the beat. "Forward on one, back on two, forward on three, pause on four, back on five, forward on six, and back on seven. Remember to take small steps" he said as he danced in place next to us. "1, 2, 3,...5, 6, 7. You've got it," he said with a smile. "Now, let's try it with music."

1, 2, 3...5, 6, 7, I smiled as I counted silently. Arty led me around the dance floor and guided me through turns, making my skirt flare.

He firmly led me through a cross body lead where he stepped to one side, and with his right hand on my back, guided me to pass in front of him, turn, and face the opposite direction. It was a smooth decisive dance pattern and made me feel as if I were a professional dancer.

"Let's do the cross body lead again, it's my favorite step," I said as I grabbed Arty's left hand. I felt exhilarated as Arty led me into another cross body lead. The music from the song, "I Could Have Danced All Night," ran through my mind.

I looked at Arty at the end of our lesson. I knew from the big smile on his face that he was pleased with himself. "Did you enjoy it?" I asked as I silently counted 1, 2, 3...5, 6, 7.... Without waiting for him to answer, I said, "I loved it! Can we book more lessons?"

Arty grabbed my hand. "Yes, absolutely. I hate to admit it, but I really enjoyed myself. I didn't believe I could learn to dance, but I got it. Eduardo is good," he said as we made our way back through the ballrooms to the reception area. Arty read the price list. "I want to buy a package of ten lessons with Eduardo," he said, handing over his credit card.

We looked at the calendar and scheduled lessons for twice a week. When we finished the first ten sessions, Arty booked another and another and another.

I remember coming home one afternoon from shopping, and Arty was waiting for me at the door. "Put the packages down quickly. Let's go. I don't want to be late for our lesson," he said as he pulled me out the door.

I laughed as we ran for a taxi. Arty wasn't sitting around watching TV anymore. He had a new excitement about him. I thought about the movie *Shall We Dance*, where a bored accountant takes dancing lessons and it changes his life.

In addition to our bi-weekly lessons, we enjoyed candlelit dinners and practiced the moves to some of our favorite Salsa rhythms. Arty led me through the cross body lead and guided me through the copa, a difficult double turn. He'd ask, "are you ready" with a big smile as he crossed my hands over his. He knew this step challenged me. I laughed as he spun me around and then reached out to pull me back into his arms. After forty-five years of marriage, dance rekindled a spark in our relationship. Arty was his old self and we were having fun again. The rhythm of 1, 2, 3... 5, 6, 7 was embedded in our souls.

We eventually arranged for Eduardo to teach us at our home, and we began to learn other ballroom dances. Two months after we began our Salsa lessons, Eduardo started us on the Fox Trot. When we finished our first Fox Trot lesson, Arty told him he felt like Fred Astaire and that I was his Ginger Rogers. Taking me in his arms, we would glide along the floor. "Slow, slow; quick, quick," he said as he guided me into a promenade. Suddenly he began to sing, "Fly me to the Moon," and pulled me closer. I felt as if I was flying to the moon; I was in heaven.

Eduardo was endearing. He enjoyed frequent dinners at our home, and I included him in many family activities including Thanksgiving at my son Mitchell's house where he taught my kids and grandkids how to dance Salsa. I started to feel close to him like he was one of my own sons. I told him that he had brought Arty back to the living. "I can't thank you enough, Eduardo. You've made Arty a new man. Before we met you Arty was very unhappy. Dancing has changed him and you did it." I hugged him tightly and told him there were great things in store for us.

Eduardo also shared his social life with us and took us to the Copacabana, the Latin Quarter, and SOBs (Sounds of Brazil) at least once a week. Through him, we were introduced to a community of people who loved to dance, a world we never knew existed.

Four days before we left for Cuba, I invited Eduardo over for a pre-Christmas dinner. He loved my home cooked meals and I made a chicken with rice dish especially for him. Eduardo smacked his lips, and as he finished the last morsel of food said, "Delicious, that was delicious. It reminded me of my mother's cooking." He placed his napkin on the table.

"Would you like an after dinner drink? I have some excellent Cognac, it goes down like velvet," Arty asked as he went to the bar.

"No thanks, I'm good," Eduardo said as he sat back in his chair and crossed his legs. "I want to tell you guys about my plans." Arty and I looked at each other. Before I had a chance to say anything, Eduardo said, "I don't know how much longer I'll be able to teach. My knees are already feeling the wear and tear." He rubbed them. "I hear the older seasoned dance instructors complain about their legs, their knees, some even complain about their backs. Most are in their early to mid forties and have nothing to show for their hard work—they'll teach until they can't anymore—and then what? What can they do? I don't want to end up like that." He took a deep breath. "I have a goal. I want to open my own studio in the next couple of years. I'm not exactly sure when, but I know I'll do it."

"What a great idea," I said as I poured myself some more wine. "You're smart to set goals for your future. I'm sure you'll make it happen. Give us a shout if you need business advice," I said as I looked at Arty. Arty didn't say a word. He continued to sip his cognac.

We said our goodbyes, wished Eduardo a Merry Christmas, and sent him off with a bottle of champagne with which to celebrate New Year's Eve.

On December 27, 2003, we boarded a flight for Havana. I could hardly contain my excitement as I placed my carry-on luggage in the overhead compartment. I took my seat and looked out the window, noticing the prop engines. "Arty, they don't fly jets to Cuba; do you think we'll be safe?" I asked looking at him for reassurance. I don't know why my anxiety had surfaced again, perhaps it was because we were traveling illegally. I started thinking my "what ifs"—What if I get sick? What if we get caught? What if we are put in jail? What if we are fined? All of Arty's objections about going to Cuba haunted me. Was he right? Should I have listened to him? No, no, I thought. Everything will be fine. I grabbed Arty's arm as we took off. Once among the clouds, I relaxed and reached into my bag for the itinerary. "Arty, our tour guide's name is Kathy and she will meet us at the airport," I said trying to get his attention away from the book he was reading. He looked at me, smiled, and went back to his book.

We arrived at Havana's Jose Marti International Airport. Much to my surprise it was very modern with stainless steel beams and enormous floor to ceiling windows. As we went through customs, we were instructed to show our passport with a blank piece of paper slipped between the pages for the custom officials to stamp. This made sure there would be no permanent record of our illegal entrance. The Cuban immigration department was aware of the politics, and the officer stamped the blank paper allowing us to enter the Communist Country.

Luckily, our entire set of luggage arrived intact. Our bags were set next to cartons tightly wrapped with cellophane tape. Each box was filled with different appliances: Sony TVs, DVD players, air conditioners, and computers. "Fragile, handle with care" was written across the boxes in bold black letters. As we grabbed our luggage, I watched the diverse Cuban people scramble to get the items that belonged to them. I was sure they were bringing these items to family members who weren't allowed to leave this Communist country. I was filled with mixed emotions: sadness for those who couldn't get out of the country and happiness that they had family or friends who brought them items we took for granted.

Arty and I wheeled our suitcases through the revolving door to the curbside. A pretty young girl in her late twenties with fair skin and light brown hair held up a sign with our names on it. We introduced ourselves and she said, "Hi, I'm Kathy. Welcome to Havana." As she helped us get our bags into the trunk, I noticed the car was a new Mercedes.

Wow, I thought. A modern hi-tech airport; a Mercedes, was this really Cuba?

Opening the back door, she asked "How was your flight? Did you have any problems?"

"No," I said as I slid across the seat to make room for Arty. "It was a very smooth flight and we breezed through customs."

"Nice car," Arty said. "I never thought we would see Cuba in a Mercedes. I like this place already."

"No, no," Kathy said smiling. "This car is only used for transferring passengers to and from the airport. We'll be taking Cuban taxis with the exception of tomorrow morning when a horse and carriage will take you around the perimeter of Old Havana."

I looked out the window at the countryside.

"How long will it take us to get to Havana?" I asked.

"Havana is only 15 kilometers from the airport, and I will point out some attractions along the way," she said as she turned to face us.

Noticing a billboard with the face of Fidel Castro, I asked what it represented.

"In our country the billboard is a form of art and depicts the revolution." Kathy said and pointed to a few along the way. She spoke perfect English.

I didn't want to get into a political debate and quickly changed the subject.

"Are there any clubs we can go to dance Salsa? Arty and I love to dance." I said, leaning forward eagerly.

"Yes, absolutely. There are many. You must go to the Casa Della Musica, it's the hottest club in Havana. I can take you there tonight," she said with a smile.

"Arty let's go, let's go tonight," I said enthusiastically tugging at his jacket.

"No. Let's get settled first. We have the whole week to dance, and I'm sure Kathy will be happy to escort us any night."

Thirty minutes later, we arrived at the five star hotel, Parque Central, our home for the week. It was in the heart of downtown Havana with El Capitol and the Gran Teatro, the home of the Ballet Nacional de Cuba and the National Opera, across the street, and a park with a marble statue of the Cuban patriot and poet, Jose Marti. Our hotel combined the elegance of colonial Spanish architecture with modern facilities, yet its classic décor clashed with the seediness of the prostitutes hanging on each corner. Directly in front of the hotel were dozens of multi-colored American cars from the 1950s, which were being used as taxis.

We entered the lobby to a familiar Latin rhythm. There was a trio of Cuban musicians serenading guests. Arty took me in his arms and we danced our way up to the registration desk. After we checked in, Kathy gave us our itinerary and said she would see us in the morning.

We went to our room and unpacked. "Arty, I left my nightshirt in Jamaica. I want to buy a new one. Maybe I can find one that has the word Cuba imprinted on it," I said as I placed my cosmetics in the bathroom.

Men, women, and children were begging outside the hotel. Walking by, I felt a pang of guilt. I was staying at this five star hotel and some people in Cuba were starving. "Give them some money—coins or dollars—anything," I said anxiously. "I feel sorry for them." Arty dug deep into his pockets and located some change and a few dollar bills. The people took the money, and I watched them bow and back away from us as they said thank you and God bless. I grabbed Arty's hand tightly and squeezed it overcome by emotion.

The environment changed dramatically as we turned the corner from the hotel. Walking under the arches, we left the grandiosity of El Capitol, the Gran Teatro, and our hotel and found ourselves in a slum-like area. The street was dirty, the shops were overcrowded, and the items filling the shelves in the stores were sparse. I couldn't find any nightshirts. Browsing, we noticed the lack of products available, whether it was drugs, cosmetics, or basic needs like band-aids, cleansers, or aspirin. Arty and I walked back to the hotel hand in hand, silently sharing a greater appreciation for the things we had.

- ♪ ♪ ♪ -

We met Kathy in the lobby after breakfast. "You carriage is waiting," she said as she shook our hands. Following behind her, I felt like Cinderella getting into my carriage with my Prince, about to be taken away to a magical land.

Kathy sat across from us as we toured Old Havana and told us how the Spanish founded the city in 1519. Designated a UNESCO World Heritage Site in 1982, it is an example of one of the finest Spanish colonial cities in the Americas. Our tour revealed sections of the original city, walls that are the modern boundary of Old Havana. The city was built in a neoclassic and baroque style, yet many of the buildings had deteriorated in the last half of the 20th century and the government was in the process of trying to restore them.

"Are there any synagogues in Old Havana?" I asked as I snapped a picture of one of the cathedrals. "My sister told me to make sure to visit one."

"Temple Adath Israel is in Old Havana, and we will be passing by it in just a minute. It dates back to the 1950s, and is hardly noticeable because of its location on the narrow crowded street," Kathy said as she pointed ahead to the building on our right.

"Can we stop for a moment? I asked.

Arty and I stepped off the carriage and told Kathy we'd only be a few minutes. We walked down a few steps and entered the sanctuary. I noticed pews on one side with a wall separating them from another set of pews located on the other side.

"Arty, this is an Orthodox temple. Orthodox Jews are the most traditional and the strictest of Jews, because they follow the interpretation of Jewish law and customs completely." Hesitating, I looked around. "Women and men are not allowed on the same side," I said pulling him back.

Arty grew up in a Reform Jewish home where they celebrated Christmas not Chanukah, whereas I grew up in a Conservative Jewish home, with parents who kept Kosher. Reform Judaism supports the basic principle of Liberalism, and a Reform Jew will follow his or her beliefs in a way that characterizes his or her freedom. Conservative Jews try to conserve the Jewish tradition, rather than reform or abandon it. Arty never learned some of the basic Jewish customs that I took for granted.

Arty continued walking. Suddenly a man with a scruffy beard, wearing a tallis (prayer shawl) and a yarmulke (skull cap), walked down from the bema (raised platform) and said, "Good Shabbas, come in."

"But women aren't allowed on that side," I said.

"You're Jewish, aren't you? Come sit." He pointed to one of

the pews.

We learned he was a visiting rabbi from Venezuela and came to Cuba each year to bring Chanukah candles and goodies back to the Jewish community in Havana. "I'm doing a mitzvah, since they can't get candles or any of the traditional items and food for the holidays," the rabbi said. "I'm like a Jewish Santa Claus."

"How many members of the congregation are there?" I asked sitting down.

"Less than 100 and the congregation is becoming smaller, as many of the Jews are migrating to Israel if they can get out of this country." Then the rabbi turned and looked at Arty.

"Did you ever lay tephillin? Would you like to?" the rabbi asked as he opened a velvet bag with the tephillin.

"No. What is tephillin? What does it mean?" Arty asked.

"According to the Talmud (Bible), tephillin is an attachment, or a pair of black leather boxes containing scrolls of parchment inscribed with biblical verses. Anyone who has the tephillin bound to his head and arm is protected from sin and binds the heart and the mind with God," the rabbi told him as he began to wrap Arty's arm with the tephillin.

I couldn't believe my eyes. I remember my brother laying tephillin when he went through a religious period during his late teen years, but Arty knew nothing of this practice.

The rabbi then placed a tallis across Arty's shoulders, a yarmulke on his head, and told him to recite after him. In my mind, Arty looked like a Bar Mitzvah boy. What a memorable experience— Arty bonding with God in Cuba. I took lots of pictures and told the rabbi that I would send him copies. We thanked him for his time and prayers, gave a contribution, and left.

We continued on our tour and Kathy briefed us on other landmarks and attractions we would see later that day and the rest of the week.

We took her to lunch at a Paladar, which was a restaurant in a private home. We learned that the only food she could afford was rice and beans. Once we heard this, we insisted that Kathy order anything on the menu that she wanted. Initially she resisted, but then ordered jumbo shrimp and rice. It was a pleasure to watch her peel the shell from the raw headless creatures, dip them in the hot sauce, and lick her lips as she devoured the last morsel of food.

We continued our tour that afternoon in a Cuban taxi and saw the Plaza de Armas, a unique and grand square, the Castillo de la Real Fuerza, a Castle of the Royal Army, the Cathedral de San Cristobal, and the Museo de la Revolución. One of the highlights of the trip was our visit to Revolution Square, where I sat on a ledge in front of the guarded offices of President Fidel Castro. It was here that Castro had addressed millions of Cuban people on special occasions. On the far side the famous image of Che Guevara overpowered the square.

"What is that?" I asked as we drove by a large pink vehicle that looked like a cross between a huge army tank and a giant Hummer.

Kathy laughed and said, "That's the 'Camel.' It got its name because of the two humps on the front and back. Its Cuba's answer to a bus and can transport more Cubans than the entire Cuban Population in the state of Florida." I was amazed as I looked at the crowd of people who depended on this means of transportation and wondered how they dealt with the intense fumes from the exhaust.

Our friends were due to arrive the next day, so Arty and I decided to check out the Casa Della Musica before their arrival.

I wanted to look extra special and went through my closet. Before we left on our trip, I had purchased special dresses for salsa dancing—halter, strapless, boat neck—they all had a flare skirt, which would swirl when Arty twirled me around. The dresses were all so pretty. They had pink and green flowers, blue and yellow stars, red and orange leaves, and a multi colored paisley background. I chose the pink and green floral for my first night on the dance floor in Cuba and held it up in front of the mirror. "Arty look how pretty this is," I said as I spun around.

It was just after 10:00 p.m., when we arrived at Casa Della Musica. The club reminded me of a dance club from the 1960s with the mirrored disco ball circling on the ceiling. The room was dark and the florescent lighting made Arty's white shirt look purple. We ordered drinks and watched as people got up to dance. Some danced by their tables and some remained in their seats swaying their bodies and clapping their hands softly to the beat of the music. After taking a few sips of my wine, I said to Arty, "Let's dance."

"No, I'm not ready," he said as he gulped his beer. "Look at everyone. They're good—*very good*. I'm not putting myself out there."

"OK, OK, I'm a little bit nervous, too. Let's order another round of drinks. It will help to relax us," I said, looking around for our waiter.

Halfway through our second round of drinks Arty said, "let's dance," and reached for my hand. Smiling, I got up and followed him to the dance floor. He led me to a dark corner and took me in his arms. He listened to the beat, 1, 2, 3...5, 6, 7, and I found myself following his lead. His smile was so big that it lit up his entire face. He radiated happiness and I was in ecstasy. We danced for about fifteen minutes and then the band took a break.

As we sat down we both wiped the sweat off our brows. I reached my hands across the table and squeezed Arty's in them. "We did it, we did it. We danced in a nightclub in Cuba. Can you believe it?" I asked as I leaned on the edge of my seat to be closer to him. Arty squeezed my hands back. He didn't say a word. He only smiled.

The next morning our friends arrived. Arty and I were still on a high but our excited moods changed quickly. "What's wrong?" I asked, greeting Mike, Marilyn, Barbara, and Steve with a hug. The grimace on their faces told me they were not happy.

"We have no luggage. They told us it should be on the next flight, but the next flight doesn't arrive until tomorrow," Mike said in disgust. "We have no clothes, no toiletries, and worse, we don't have our medication."

"Calm down," Arty said. "We can try and get some basics now and I can lend you a toothbrush, toothpaste, and deodorant."

Hoping this would not put a damper on our trip, we went to the marketplace and to a local drugstore. We couldn't find any medications close to what they needed, but we were able to find them clean underwear.

The next day they went to the airport in search of their luggage. Mike argued with the authorities, but it became clear that they were powerless to do anything. Kathy told us it was a common occurrence for the airport to misplace tourist's luggage. "You and Arty were lucky," she said as she tried to use her influence with the baggage handlers.

My friends didn't receive their luggage until the day before they left Cuba. After two days of being disgruntled, they decided to be good sports and have a good time. We enjoyed dinners at Paladars, visited Ernest Hemingway's house, spent a day at a coffee plantation one hour from Havana, where we were serenaded by two Cuban old timers, and enjoyed a typical Cuban meal of homemade rice and beans with chicken. One of the highlights of our trip was a performance by the Buena Vista Social Club. In the 1940s, the Buena Vista Social Club had been a popular location for Cuban artists to meet and play their music. Fifty years after the club closed, it inspired a recording named The Buena Vista Social Club, which achieved international success.

The Buena Vista Social Club performed at the historic luxury Hotel Nacional located on the Malecón. The Hotel Nacional had opened its doors in 1930 and was considered a number one travel spot for Americans before the embargo. It was said that Frank Sinatra had sat at the bar tasting rum punches and that Sir Winston Churchill had been spotted puffing good Havana cigars. Autographed photos of Marlon Brando, Rita Hayworth, Ava Gardner, Tyrone Power, Errol Flynn, and the Prince of Wales line the hotel walls of the Salon de la Fama.

"Look Arty, there's Nat King Cole's photo and Fred Astaire's," I said. "I can't believe all of these famous people stayed here." I tried to read every caption, but Arty pulled me along.

"Come on, let's go," he said. "I don't want to be late for

the show."

Walking to the ballroom, I noticed an elderly woman sitting in a chair facing a TV camera with bright flood lights shining down on her. Her hair was matted down and a multi colored shawl was wrapped around her slumped shoulders. A young woman holding a microphone was interviewing her. "She must be someone important," I said to Arty and stopped to ask the security guard.

"That's Omara Portunondo. She's one of the original members of the Buena Vista Social Club and she's singing here tonight," he told us as he waved us on.

"Wow. She's the lead singer? I'm surprised she's not in a costume for TV," I said as we picked up our pace.

We entered the corridor of the ballroom. There were Christmas trees with red and white flickering lights and poinsettias sitting on the registration table that warmed the stone walled room. The line to check in was very long and moved slowly. There was heavy security. Arty and I waited patiently.

After entering the ballroom we quickly found our seats. Our friends sat at the table next to us. We introduced ourselves to people sitting around us; most were from the United States. There was a couple from Texas, two couples were from Florida and another couple was from California. I finished my dinner and took some time to look around. I learned that Fidel Castro had banned the celebration of Christmas when he came into power, but lifted the ban in 1997 to honor the visit of Pope John Paul II. It was hard to believe that Christmas was relatively new in this country as the room was festive and sparkled with garlands, holiday lights and ornaments.

The room grew quiet when the Master of Ceremonies introduced the Buena Vista Social Club. First, they played as a group and then Omara Portunondo came onto the stage. I couldn't believe she was the same woman I had seen being interviewed earlier. Her big smile radiated energy and her presence lit up the stage like a bolt of lightening. She wore a long colorful skirt with a ruffled blouse trimmed with the colors of the rainbow and a brightly colored head piece resembling a turban. As she moved like a gazelle, her voice resonated throughout the ballroom. She held a hollowed out gourd and rubbed the notches with a stick as she belted out songs. She engaged the audience by passing out tambourines, maracas, and small gourds. Everyone stretched their arms in hopes of catching one of the instruments. It was a magical evening; we danced, we sang and swayed back and forth to the infectious Latin rhythms, not wanting the night to end.

I sat in awe as I watched the remarkable concert. They were the most astonishing musical group and everything about them—their talent, their energy, their very presence—moved me. The room was filled with smiling faces. People were tapping their hands on the table in tempo to the beat, while others danced in the aisle. These veteran musicians were still bringing people together and spreading joy. They weren't retired. They were a great source of pleasure to all ages, and they continued to give back. As I clapped, I thought, retirement isn't about sitting around. We should use our golden years to reap the rewards of sharing happiness with others.

I felt an inner surge of joy and wanted to hold on to this beautiful country and the beautiful people who lived there. We all stood up as Omara sang the song "Guantanamera" ("Girl from Guantánamo").

This is Cuba's best known song and is also considered patriotic. We waved our arms and moved our hips to the sensual rhythm. "Encore, encore," everyone shouted as the music came to an end.

We couldn't stop talking about the wonderful evening. We had seen the Buena Vista Social Club; my sister had told me about them but I never thought we'd see their performance. "Arty, they were amazing," I said as we left the hotel. He pulled me toward a taxi. "They were beyond amazing!" he said. Little did we know it, but our experience with the joy of Salsa dancing, the allure of the Buena Vista Social Club, and the sensual rhythms of Cuba, would soon lead us to a new chapter in our lives.

— ♪ ♪ ♪ —

Cha Cha

The Cha Cha started as a new Mambo rhythm,
danced on the off beat rather than the traditional downbeat.
Among the many representations of the Mambo,
one was called the "Chatch," which involved
three quick changes of weight preceded by two slow steps.
By the early 1950s, this representation developed
into a new dance and became known as the Cha Cha.

Soho Dance

Having caught the "Dance Fever,"
the energetic rhythm of the Cha Cha took us into
a world that changed our lives forever.

"Eduardo, Eduardo," I shouted excitedly into the phone. Our flight had just landed, and I immediately dialed Eduardo's phone number as I got into the car that took us home. "We danced all over Cuba—the restaurants, the streets, the clubs—and New Year's Eve was a dance marathon. When my feet ached I took my shoes off." I laughed aloud. "Eduardo, are you listening?"

"Yes, yes, that's great," he said. His voice sounded cheerful and I sensed he was happy to hear from us. "I missed you guys and can't wait to see you. Are you going to take another lesson?"

"Of course we are! I'll call you tomorrow," I paused. "By the way Happy New Year. It's going to be a dancing year, you can bet on it!" I hung up and squeezed Arty's hand.

After speaking with Eduardo, I thought how strange it was that

I called him before I called my kids, but I rationalized it by realizing that dancing had been on my mind our entire trip.

Eduardo came to our home two days later and we began our lessons again. Arty and I had booked a cruise to Scandinavia and Russia for the following June and before we left, we wanted to improve our dance repertoire as well as learn new ballroom dances.

"Arty, let's show Eduardo how we danced in Cuba," I said as I grabbed him. Arty followed my lead and took me in his arms firmly placing the palm of his right hand just below my shoulder blades. I looked at Eduardo and said, "Music maestro." Eduardo turned up the CD player and took a seat on the couch directly in front of us. After we danced through our routine Eduardo called out, "Bravo, bravo." Arty and I looked at each other proudly and took a bow.

"We're pros at Salsa, so what's next?" I asked.

"It's up to the both of you, whatever you want. Let's brush up on your Fox Trot and then we can move on to some new sequences. When you're ready we can tackle a new dance," he said as he looked through his own collection, thumbing his iPod.

Arty arched his back slightly and pressed me into his right arm as he proceeded to lead me around the room. Slow, slow, quick, quick, he repeated quietly as the crooner sang "*On The Road to Mandalay.*" When we neared the corner, Eduardo introduced us to the side sway move.

"This movement is made up of sideway movements to the slow, slow, quick, quick count of the Fox Trot," he explained. "The slow counts are side steps, and the quick, quick is a side chasse. This step can be danced without any turn or with a slight turn to the left or right. It's a good way to avoid bumping into people on a crowded dance floor." Taking me in his arms, Eduardo said, "Watch me Arty."

After we practiced a few of these new moves, Eduardo promised to teach us a version of the Hustle for our next lesson. "I know about that dance. I remember the iconic scene of John Travolta raising his right arm up and down across his chest in the movie *Saturday Night Fever*. I'm excited to learn the dance," I said as I tried to mimic his moves.

Eduardo smiled at me and took a seat on one of our stools at the counter.

"I want to update you on my goal to open my own studio." He paused. "I mentioned my plans to a couple who teach with me. They expressed an interest and we had a few meetings. I'm not sure where to go from here."

"Eduardo, this sounds good," I said as I patted him on his back. I turned and looked at Arty. "Arty," I asked, "what do you think? Can you give Eduardo any advice?"

"Get more information," Arty said. He stood up from the couch. "Find out what they really want. Do they want to be partners? Do they have money to invest? Do they have a following? I'll give you a list of questions to ask them," he said and grabbed a pen and pad from the desk.

"See you Friday," I said. "I'm going to listen to the Bee Gees before our lesson so I can acquaint myself with the song 'Night Fever.' Arty you'll be my John Travolta." I kissed Eduardo good-by.

We continued our bi-weekly lessons for the next couple of

months. Eduardo taught us the Hustle and the Cha Cha, my favorite dances after Salsa. I was happy with the variety of dances we were learning, and we worked hard to perfect our steps for our upcoming cruise. We continued to go to dance clubs, sometimes with Eduardo, sometimes just the two of us. We had a regular dance schedule: Tuesday night was dancing at the Copa, Wednesday was the Latin Quarter, and Fridays we went to SOBs.

It was early April and we were on our way home from the Copa.

"What a crowd they had," I said holding Arty's hand. I can't believe so many people came out to dance on this rainy night. There must have been a thousand people there." Arty looked at me and smiled. My mind raced. I suddenly felt impulsive.

"Arty, let's open a dance studio. It will be fun, challenging, keep us busy—and give us the opportunity to dance anytime we want to. Don't you think it would be so gratifying to share our passion with others?" I said. "Don't you think it's a great idea? We can open the studio with Eduardo."

Arty let go of my hand and said, "You're crazy. There's no way I am opening a dance studio. I don't know anything about the dance business."

"Yes, you do. You had a client who owned a studio and you helped her become a big success. You can do it. I know you can."

Arty shook his head as we got out of the cab, repeating, "You're crazy."

But I couldn't let it go. "When we take our lesson tomorrow, I'm going to discuss it with Eduardo," I said as I pushed the button for the elevator. Arty didn't say another word.

The red numbers on my digital clock showed that it was 2:00 a.m. Our apartment was quiet except for the sound of Arty snoring. How could he sleep so soundly? Why didn't he feel like I did? I wanted to sleep but I was restless. I tried to find a comfortable spot and turned my body from one side to the other. I closed my eyes and lay on my back as if I were in Shavasana at the end of my yoga class. Listen to your breath, I thought. That's what Myra would tell me. But I couldn't quiet my mind. All I could think about was the dance studio. I placed my hands on my stomach. The rise and fall of my abdomen soothed me. I went into a dreamlike state. I began to see images of bright shiny colors flashing before me; red, green, bright yellow, blue, pink, purple, orange—there were hundreds of colors. I shook my head thinking it was my imagination, but they kept coming and moved faster as if they were beams of light. Was it a big rainbow? I arched my back to get closer to the imagery. Then I heard music. It was Salsa music vibrating in my ears. Was this a creation of my imagination or was it real? I released my mind from reality and dreamt that I was in the ballroom of my new dance studio watching women in multi-colored skirts that swirled like whirling dervishes, as their partners took them across the floor in cross body leads and spun them in under-arm turns. I wanted to join them and swayed my hips to the Latin rhythm. My hot pink Salsa dress glowed as Arty guided me through his own choreography. The room lit up as the wall to wall mirrors reflected the dancers and the glitter of the ballroom. I was consumed with happiness as Arty spun me into the Copa. I reached for his hand to pull me back from the double turn. "Arty catch me, I'm falling, fallinggggg..." I woke with a start. Where am I? Holding my hand over my open mouth, I sat up quickly. For a moment I thought that I was hallucinating. I must wake Arty, I thought, I must tell him about my dream. I looked at him sleeping peacefully and part of me dared not disturb his peacefulness, but then my impulses took over and I nudged him gently. Just as I raised my elbow to nudge him again, Arty let out a big grunt.

"Arty, Arty wake up. I saw our dance studio," I said. "I saw our dance studio in my dream; it was filled with lots of dancers!" I continued to tug at him. Slowly, Arty came to life, puckered his lips, and held out his arms, he wanted to make love. I ignored him and blurted out again, "Our dance studio was full of people dancing."

Arty opened his eyes, blinking to counter his disorientation. Still not clear what was taking place, he reached over for a kiss. I put my hand softly over his lips and said, "Not now, I have to talk to you. We're going to open a dance studio; I saw it in my dreams."

When the realization hit him that I did not want to have sex, Arty looked at me and said once again, "You're crazy!" He immediately lay back down, pulled the blanket over his head, and shrieked, "I'm not listening."

"But Arty," I tried to pull the covers from him, "I know it'll work." He turned his back to me. I lay there quietly and thought, "We'll discuss it in the morning when Eduardo arrives."

Eduardo showed up early for our lesson. We spent a little more than an hour dancing, and when we finished, I asked Eduardo to sit down with us. Without considering my husband's feelings, I said, "Arty and I are thinking of opening a dance studio. Are you interested?"

"What? You're what?" he repeated as if he didn't understand what I had just said.

"We want to open a dance studio with you. What do you think?" I asked.

Eduardo looked at me and then at Arty. "Are you sure you want to do this? I would love nothing more than to open a dance studio with you guys," he said as he stood up and walked around the room.

"Arty, see, I told you Eduardo would do it. Let's open a dance studio together. You have the business head, I'll do the marketing, and Eduardo can be the artistic director in charge of the teachers." I hesitated and took a breath. "He knows the dance side, you know the business side, and I will brand it as I did with ADL & Co. It's a win win proposition," I said as I got up to get a pad and make some notes.

Arty continued to resist. "No, I do not want to open a dance studio. You do it with Eduardo."

"Come on Arty. It'll be a great adventure, I know we can do it, I know we can," I said confidently as I began to scribble some notes.

"I repeat! I am not opening a dance studio," he said loudly and walked into the bedroom.

Eduardo followed behind Arty, his black eyes wide with excitement. Standing in the doorway, he said, "I believe we *can* do it. I know a lot of teachers who might be interested in coming with us, and I have lots of students who will follow me."

Arty turned to Eduardo. "Get this straight; I do not want to open a dance studio. I have no desire to deal with running a business again. I would have to worry about paying the rent and the bills, but even more important, I vowed never to have employees again."

I believed that Arty wanted to open a studio but was afraid

he'd fail. I knew he was worried about mounting bills, harassment by bill collectors, and employees who were unreliable. I remember Arty continually telling me that everything revolves around money. His exact words were: It's always about the money. Money was something he worried about constantly, and now that he had finally reached a stage in his life where he didn't have to worry, why should he take a chance? But I had confidence in him. In my heart I knew that together we would build a successful dance studio. I just had to convince him.

I went to Eduardo who stood in our hallway, and said, "Leave Arty alone. I'll talk to him."

Eduardo had great respect for Arty and didn't want to push him into anything he didn't want to do, but even he persisted. "Rosann, I know we can do this. This will be great for all of us."

I knew that Eduardo had a different agenda than we did. He was in his thirties and we were seniors. He had everything to gain, but we had a lot to lose. As I listened to him, I visualized him kicking back with his feet up on an executive desk, smoking a Monte Cristo cigar after he finished directing a cadre of instructors on the syllabus for each class. I laughed to myself as I pictured the holes on the soles of his shoes that were resting on the desk. What did the holes in his shoes symbolize, I wondered. "We'll see you tomorrow," I said. Kissing me on the cheek, Eduardo left.

I walked into the bedroom. Arty was lying on the bed reading. I sat down on the edge next to him. "Arty, I didn't mean to disregard your feelings, but I feel strongly about opening a dance studio," I said as I rubbed his thigh. "Why are you so opposed?"

Arty placed his book on the nightstand. His voice softened, but he looked uncomfortable. "I always wanted to please you, but felt I never gave you enough. I want to give you more, but I'm concerned." He reached for my hand. "I'm not sure this is the time to take this kind of risk. We'd have to take money from our retirement to fund it. I'm a risk taker, but opening a dance studio could be a bigger risk than I'd like to take." He paused. "I want to give you more, but I must consider our future." He patted my hand and gently placed it back on my lap.

I understood his conflict. "But Arty," I said. "We're in this together. I wouldn't push you to do this if I thought we'd fail. We must plan to do something with the rest of our lives—sitting around watching TV or going to dance clubs doesn't do it—we need more." I stood up and pleaded, "Please, please, I know we can make this a success."

Arty gazed into my eyes. He took a deep breath. "Ro, I'm still not convinced it's the right thing for us to do," he said as he sat up.

"Arty, you're a business man and a good one. We built two businesses together successfully. This will be no different and we'll have more fun." I hesitated. I looked for any hook, and suddenly, I remembered our payout from J. H Cohn—we only had five years left on our payout. That's it, that's it, I thought. "Arty, we only have five years left on our payout from J. H. Cohn," I said letting my tone lift with enthusiasm. "Our dance studio will be our five-year plan. When the J. H. Cohn money stops our dance studio will feed us. You can't say no to that." I sat back down on the bed. "What do I have to do to convince you?"

Arty's face relaxed and I noticed a slight upturn to his lips. "You have a good point." As his smile got bigger he said, "Hug me,

Ro, and don't let go."

We lay in each other's arms. The room was quiet except for the sound of the inhalation and exhalation of our breath. My head rested on his chest and I felt deeply connected to him, as if our souls had united. We didn't let go until Arty sat up. He cupped my face with his hands, took a deep breath and said, "OK, OK, I'll do it. Let's open a dance studio." In my heart I knew that the five-year plan wasn't the deciding factor, it was really just his lifelong desire to please me.

When Eduardo arrived the next morning, I told him the news. He was overjoyed with delight and reached out to hug Arty. "This is great news, I can't believe it," he said.

"Don't hug me, just work hard," Arty said as he pulled away from Eduardo's outstretched arms. "Most of this will be on your plate," Arty said. "You'll have to find *good* teachers—teachers with a following who know how to engage the students. They are the key to making this a success. What assurance can you give me that this will happen?" Arty hesitated. "Set up a meeting with the couple you told me about. I want to talk to them and see if they are real."

"I'll call them now. When do you want to meet?" Eduardo asked as he reached for the cell phone in his bag.

"Tomorrow morning," Arty said.

Eduardo confirmed the meeting for 10:00 a.m., the next day. "Good, now let's get started. We have a lot of work to do," Arty said handing each of us a legal sized pad. Eduardo took the pad as he shook Arty's hand and said, "I'm ready, partner."

"We'll begin by writing up the business plan." Arty said as he took an outline to write a plan out of the desk drawer. "Rosann and I will do some research on the Internet and see if there are any studios for sale. One option might be to buy an existing studio with a following. I will also set up a meeting with my former dance studio client and seek her advice." Arty paused. Squinting, he put the top of his pen to his forehead and said, "But I don't want to eliminate the possibility of additional partners who have money to invest. It will take away some of our financial burden."

Collectively, we all had the same vision—to do whatever it took to open a successful dance studio. We spent considerable time discussing our options, and set a goal to open by the first of the New Year. That gave us eight months.

"Eduardo, continue to speak with teachers and set up interviews. Ro, you write a marketing plan focusing on how to attract students. I'll do a budget and get the financials in order," Arty said as he wrote up a to do list.

I couldn't get the smile off my face. I was a sixty-two-year-old grandmother opening a Latin ballroom dance studio. I was in disbelief, yet felt tremendously empowered. A new and exciting chapter of my life was about to begin in my "Golden Years."

The next morning we met with Steve and Susan. Steve specialized in Latin dances: Salsa, Cha Cha, Merengue, Tango, Rhumba, and had a big following. Susan's specialty was the Hustle and the Fox Trot. They were very anxious to partner with us, as they were unhappy as employees at a dance studio in Murray Hill. "We have loyal students and our boss is reaping the benefits financially," Steve said leaning back in his chair. "I can help Eduardo organize the teachers and the syllabus for the various dances. Susan can help Rosann get the word out about the studio."

"Sounds good to me," Arty said as he stood up. "Steve, you can begin to talk up your student base, and Susan, you can check on where we can rent space and begin teaching immediately. I'll figure out the money piece; let's meet again in two days."

We liked Steve and Susan and believed that they would be a great addition to our team, but during our second meeting things didn't go the way we planned.

They wanted to own 50% of the business without investing any money. "Our students are worth something," Steve said.

Arty explained that they would own phantom stock which gave them a piece of the profits after a certain amount of money had been earned. "What's a phantom stock?" Susan asked. "Does that mean we own a piece of the company?"

"Not the way you think of owning a company," Arty explained. "It's based on our profits. If the company does well, the phantom stock will give both of you cash or a stock bonus to be paid out at a specified time, but only after we reach our financial goal. I will have my attorney draw up an agreement stating our monetary goals and when the bonus will be given." Arty laid his pen down on the table. "This is a great offer and Eduardo has the same deal."

Susan looked at Steve, then at Arty. Her mouth fell open and her eyes welled up with tears. "This is unacceptable," she said wiping her eyes. "We want a real partnership. We want to own 50% of the company, not as phantoms. I want my name on the agreement to say partner."

"C'mon Steve, let's go," Susan said as she stood up.

We never saw them again.

- ♪ ♪ ♪ -

We sat around the table and brainstormed. "Eduardo, do you think you can do this without other partners?" Arty asked as he scribbled on his pad. Without hesitation Eduardo said, "I can do it...I know I can do it. I know *we* can do it."

"OK, OK," Arty said as he began to update our new to do list. "We should start to look for space, but first I will check out the studio that's for sale in Lower Manhattan, that I located on the Internet. I will make an appointment to meet with the owner. I will also visit with my former client who owns the dance studio nearby on the Upper West Side." Arty exercised his power as the boss and set the tone for us to go forward. He was back in business.

"Eduardo, keep interviewing dance instructors. Rosann, you'll come with me and we'll regroup in a couple of days."

We arrived at the dance studio in Lower Manhattan the next day at five in the afternoon. I turned to Arty as we stepped off the elevator. "This place is not for us," I said as I walked into the reception area. "It's prime time and I don't hear any music; there is no one dancing. I feel like I'm in a morgue. Let's go," I said as I turned around to leave.

"No, don't be so impulsive. We don't have any facts. Just because the walls are dingy grey, the carpets worn and tattered, and the studio has a musty smell, you shouldn't reject the place. These details are aesthetics and can be fixed," Arty said as he pulled me back.

Instinctively, though, I knew I was right. The owner's records were poor. He couldn't give us precise financials; his database didn't track the number of new or repeat students, there was no follow up system, and he wanted too much money. As we left, I remembered a phrase from one of Arty's former partners: "When the fish stinks, it starts at the head." I laughed to myself as I stepped into the elevator.

I leaned my head on Arty's shoulder as we rode in the taxi back home. My studio wouldn't be like that, I thought. I want it to have life, to have energy. I want it to be a place where people can go to learn to dance, rehearse for a performance, or just find a place to escape. My space will radiate happiness. I remembered a friend of mine, who owns a number of restaurants, telling me every guest that dined in his restaurants should feel as if they were transported to a new destination. I wanted my students to experience that. I wanted them to feel that they were embarking on an exciting journey. My studio will be a step out of the ordinary, I thought. It will promote health, happiness, and camaraderie through dance. I closed my eyes and visualized hundreds of smiling faces gliding along the dance floor of my ballroom. Ladies in formal gowns and men in tuxedos passed in front of me. Music rang in my ears, beautiful music. "Wake up, wake up," Arty said as he shook me gently. "We're home."

We continued with our plan and met with Arty's former client who liked our idea yet advised us to include a children's program on our schedule, since it could be a profit center. Arty liked that idea.

Eduardo reported on his interviews with possible dance instructors. "One of my friends is an excellent instructor in Argentine Tango, another is a champion Salsa dancer with a big following. Both are interested in talking more," he said and handed us headshots of both.

250

See it in your minds eye - The Child, emotional, laughter

"That's a good start. I want to meet them," Arty said.

As Eduardo picked up his phone to call them, Arty reached for the palm pilot on his desk. "I'm calling a friend who is a commercial real estate broker. I think we should start to look for a rental space and forego buying an existing studio," he said. "We should concentrate on the area of 23rd Street and below; there are fewer studios there, access to good public transportation, and heavy pedestrian traffic at night." He paused. "We are more apt to find an open loft space downtown with a more affordable rent than we can find uptown."

After Arty made an appointment to meet with the broker, he said, "Ro, now it's your turn. You need to do what you do best—network and get the buzz out."

"But we don't have the space yet, we don't have a name, how do I do that?" I asked.

"That's your job. You'll figure it out. I don't want to hear any what ifs this time!" Eduardo left and Arty went to the gym.

Fear took over and I began to doubt my abilities. Why now? I thought. I want to open a dance studio—I *know* it will be a success. I walked to the window and stared at the Hudson River. The water glistened from the sun's rays, calming me. Kids played on the newly built Pier I in Riverside Park South that jutted into the Hudson. Some children were skateboarding, some threw a ball around, while others attempted to bump and grind with their hula-hoops. In my imagination, the children became adults and their cut off shorts and sun dresses turned into sparkling costumes. They were dancing! They were dancing on the pier. That's it! That's it! I thought. I'll arrange for Eduardo to give complimentary dance lessons on the pier. I had a good connection with the parks department. Flopping down on the couch, I reached for the phone. I could barely contain my enthusiasm as I dialed my contact's number.

Even though we didn't have a space or a name for our studio, I created our first program in the summer of 2004 and called it "Let's Dance." My graphic designer printed flyers that I distributed throughout the park and the surrounding apartment buildings promoting our complimentary dance lessons in the park every Sunday night beginning at 6:00 p.m. throughout the summer into late September.

For that first evening, I wanted to make a good impression and look youthful. So I ran to the Betsy Johnson store on Columbus Avenue and bought a black mini skirt with pink ribbons dotting the short hemline and a black tee shirt. The first evening was a tremendous success. I felt completely in control as I stood on a raised platform at the end of the pier with a microphone in hand, welcoming everyone to our Let's Dance program with the setting sun as a spotlight. As I spoke, my exhilaration heightened my senses and I moved my feet to the rhythm of the DJ's music which softly played throughout my speech. After the introduction, the DJ turned up the volume, and Eduardo and I took to the center stage. We danced a hot, sexy Salsa, demonstrating the steps the participants were about to learn. My feet barely touched the cement surface as Eduardo twirled me around. The lyrics from the Lionel Richie song, "Dancing in the Dark" filled my head—only in my mind I changed Dark to Park. We took a bow and I bathed in the wonderfully loud applause.

More than 100 people attended our lessons each week. We

offered complimentary lessons upon the opening of our studio to anyone who joined our email list and by the end of the summer we had close to 1000 names. The buzz was out.

- ♪ ♪ ♪ -

Eduardo continued interviewing teachers while we continued to look for space. After seeing more than one dozen spaces, we finally found one that fulfilled all of our needs. It was a 5500 square foot loft in a nine-floor, cast iron landmark building located in Soho. We met with the landlord and the deal was sealed with a handshake. A copy of the lease was sent to our lawyer, and we set a tentative date for the build-out to begin in late September or early October. To our favor, we wouldn't have to start paying rent until December.

Arty and I smiled at one another as we left the landlord's office. "Nice guy," I said to Arty as we walked through the crowd toward the subway one block away. Arty nodded and said, "I have the name— Soho Dance. Soho Dance," he repeated. I squeezed his hand tightly. Soho Dance it was. We knew we had made the right decision.

"December is not that far off. Eduardo and I will oversee the construction, but you must continue to build a database and have students ready to take lessons the minute we open our doors," he told me.

We interviewed a number of architects and hired a man in his late forties who specialized in designing Greek Orthodox Churches. The pictures of his award winning designs expressed a skill and creativity that represented the similarities and dissimilarities of diverse cultures, yet were ethnic in nature. We wanted the same

253

look for our Latin ballroom dance studio, in order to create drama, excitement, and the magnetism to attract people from all societies.

We spent most of our days in our raw space. Stepping over some debris from the demolition, I picked up the blueprints and taped them to one of the walls that eventually would be mirrored. "Look, the blueprint designates four studios. How will we separate them?" I asked the architect.

"They will be separated through theatrical drapery, similar to the curtains that normally hang between the stage and the audience, only your drapes will be hung on heavy tracks to be pulled and tied back when you want the use of the whole ballroom," he said as he showed us a picture in a book. Impulsively, I bent my knees, placed one foot behind the other, and curtsied as if I had just finished a dance performance. "I love it," I said and continued to look at the plans.

The build-out was a huge job. Arty and Eduardo ordered hi-tech lighting that changed colors, wall to wall mirrors, stainless steel sinks on marble pedestals for the bathrooms, computers for the front and back office, and contracted a carpenter to custom build the reception desk. The walls were to be painted white with the exception of the main ballroom. For the ballroom, we hired an artist to paint the New York skyline and boldly graffiti our name: SOHO DANCE in bright yellow and orange, outlined in black on the walls. With the help of SOHO DANCE, we were about to Cha Cha our way through our retirement and beyond.

- ♪ ♪ ♪ -

Hustle

The Hustle is a catchall name for a variety
of disco dances that were popular in the 1970s.
The Hustle, an offshoot of the Mambo, began in
Hispanic communities in New York City and Florida.
Eventually, a line dance with a Salsa-like foot rhythm
and some fusion with Swing became known
as the "New York" Hustle.

A Blast of Snow!

We danced the Hustle to open our doors
in grandiose style
to a winter wonderland!

I sat down and began to enter the long list of names into my database from our Let's Dance program in Riverside Park the week before. After a few minutes I looked up and saw Arty talking with the architect. I laughed as I heard Arty say, "We don't need stained glass windows; we're building a Latin Ballroom Dance studio, not a Greek Orthodox Church."

Eduardo was giving a lesson to one of his loyal students amidst the dust. A powdery film filled the area as Eduardo took his student through turns, but they didn't seem to mind the residue and continued dancing.

I was worrying how to broaden my outreach. Riverside Park was a good start, but I needed more options. I slumped in my chair and then realized, Why not do for Soho Dance what I did at ADL &

Co.? I built that business through networking; I could do the same thing for Soho Dance! I reached for a flyer that someone had sent to me. In big bold letters the headline read, "The Power of Networking: Your Road To Business Success." A cocktail reception was being held the following week at a bank in Midtown. I immediately picked up the phone to RSVP. I heard a dial tone. My voice echoed throughout the studio as I yelled, "We have phone service!" I left a message, marked my calendar, and made a note to bring lots of business cards. Maybe I'll bring some pictures too, I thought, and I dragged the curser to iPhoto. The slide show from our Let's Dance program was like watching a movie about dance. There were almost 100 people, all strangers dancing with one another and smiling as they learned a basic routine. I laughed aloud as I saw one person dancing with her dog. This was great! The pictures would help sell lessons. Where else can I promote the studio, I asked myself. I remembered meeting the director from a local YMCA at a recent luncheon I had attended in Soho. The YMCA would be a good venue to offer classes. I rummaged through my Rolodex file and found his business card.

"I'd like to meet with you to discuss a new program for your members," I said as I began to print some of the photos. The director gave me the phone number for the Y's program manager and I confirmed a meeting with her for the next day. "I'll bring you a slide show that demonstrates a sample of a program that we can teach at the Y."

"I'm looking forward to meeting you," she said. "Have the receptionist buzz me when you arrive. See you at 10:00 a.m. tomorrow."

We met the next morning. She loved our program and scheduled us to start teaching every Saturday beginning in January. "I will publicize Soho Dance in our directory as well as distribute flyers to our members," she told me. We shook hands and I left feeling elated.

Eduardo was now interviewing prospective new teachers and someone to run the front desk. Because they didn't have to be partners, his job was easier. Arty was still working with the architect and I continued my search to plant seeds for students. Ultimately Eduardo hired a receptionist and nine teachers with Arty's approval.

The build-out was slower than we anticipated, as we had to work around the unreliable schedules of the workmen and back-ordered mirrors, lighting, bathroom fixtures, and other necessary items. It was the middle of October and we set December 1st as our tentative opening date.

"The movie, *Shall We Dance* is opening the last week in October in theaters throughout New York," I said to Eduardo and Arty as I showed them the ad in the newspaper. "We should do guerilla marketing."

"What's guerilla marketing?" Eduardo asked.

"It's different than traditional marketing. It's a promotion, where the potential buyers are targeted when they least expect it, thus creating an immediate buzz. We can hire students to stand at the theaters close to Soho and have them hand out flyers offering free lessons when we open on December 1st," I said. "We are going to open December 1st, right?" I looked at Arty.

"That's the plan, but anything can happen, so I can't be sure."

Arty said as he scratched his head. "I like your idea of guerilla marketing and it won't cost us a lot. Set that up, but be sure the flyer boldly states they *must* call to schedule their lesson in just in case we miss our target opening date."

I arrived early at the bank in midtown for the networking event. A short slender woman with brown hair dressed in a navy blue suit greeted me. "Did you pre-register?" she asked as she looked down at her list.

"Yes," I said and gave her my name.

"Welcome to 'Building Your Business Through Networking.' My name is Liz. I am the Founder and Executive Director of this new organization," she said as she gave me my badge. "We are an exclusive networking group. Membership is limited to one person per industry and new business leads are mandatory at each meeting."

Smiling, I pinned my badge to the right side of my lapel and walked toward a table filled with soft drinks, a fruit platter, and cookies. As I poured myself a glass of water I looked around the room.

The reception took place in the lobby of the bank and was filled with about twenty young professionals talking quietly while exchanging business cards. There were twenty-five folding chairs arranged in a semi circle in the center of the room. This is a perfect group, I thought. It encompassed young men and woman who would enjoy the physical outlet of dance. As I made my way toward the crowd, Liz instructed everyone to take a seat, and invited each of us to make a brief business presentation. There was a lawyer, realtor, insurance salesman, accountant, and other professionals—

only one per industry as she had said. I listened intently to each presentation, and when it was my turn I passed out the pictures I had brought. I assured everyone that they would learn a basic routine during their first lesson. "Our artistic director, Eduardo, is the best in his field and our teachers are all specialists in their own right," I said as I continued to pass around the photos. Suddenly a young man with dark brown wavy hair dressed in a grey pin striped suit blurted out, "I agree. I know Eduardo. I took lessons from him and he's wonderful. I learned to dance in my very first lesson; in fact, I am still taking lessons from him."

My mouth fell open. I couldn't have planned this better than if I had planted a shill in the audience. "See, I speak the truth, and I have never seen this young man before," I said and everyone laughed.

Before I left, I spoke with Liz and decided to join the group. She asked if we would be willing to donate our space for their Christmas party. "Can you do it on December 14th? I will supply the food and drink. All we need is the space and you can give everyone a lesson," she said as she took out her day planner.

"Absolutely. We'll be glad to donate our space," I said as I shook her hand. "We'll make it a fun party and more important your members will learn to dance!"

"Arty, Arty I have donated our dance studio for a Christmas party to a networking group I've joined. We'll be open by December 14th—this won't be a problem, right?" I thought we'd shift the students that would call about lessons to the 14th—that would become our new hard deadline. Again I looked to Arty for confirmation. It was out of my control, but Arty would make it happen for me. I knew he would!

"I think so, but I am not making any promises. We are already into the second week of November. I can't control shipments and I can't control the workmen," he said as he looked at the list of things that had to be done. "Here...look at my list; we are waiting for a new air conditioning system to be installed, the lights are back-ordered, as are the bathroom fixtures, we can't open without toilets. The carpenter is working diligently to get our reception desk complete but the marble top is on special order. The drapes should be here but we can open without them. The last thing to be done is the floor. It must be stripped and painted with polyurethane. This can't be done until everything else is complete, because we can't walk on them for three days. There are no guarantees."

"But...but, I promised. You *must* make it happen. We *must* open by December 14th," I said looking at the calendar. "It's not that far off and we are halfway through with the build-out." I looked around the barren space and watched the workmen sweep up the debris and dump it into the big dumpster in the middle of the floor. They worked in slow motion. I wanted to kick them in the ass, but restrained myself. I simply refused to believe we wouldn't open by Dec. 14th.

I focused instead on finding students. I looked through my contacts from the networking meeting and spotted a banker. Why would bankers want to dance? I called her up. It turned out she was looking for a way to motivate her sales team and said, "I think dance might be a healthy way to inspire my group. I hold monthly meetings and I have an opening in January. Can you do something for us?" she asked.

"I have some ideas. Let me get back to you with a program that I would deem appropriate for your group," I told her while making some notes. "Something different, something fun, yet something that'll relate to their jobs."

I remember feeling charged up after the call. I stared out the window. What would stimulate people who work in the corporate world? What would alleviate their stress and motivate them to be better sales people? How could I apply the lead-follow technique of dance to people who wore pin stripe suits? I watched the hoards of people with sullen faces walking quickly down Broadway. It was as if they were rushing—but rushing where? I wanted to yell out, "You Should Be Dancing." Suddenly I imagined that Broadway had become a stage—a big stage. Everyone grabbed a partner and began to dance. Hanging on to the sill, I leaned further out the window to get a better look and watched the crowd move effortlessly towards Prince Street and continue toward Spring street. Salsa music filled my ears and the street swarmed with dancers. People teamed up— the leader led and the partner followed. I smiled as I swayed back and forth and envisioned a harmonious team. The loud honking of horns startled me. I looked around the studio. It was quiet except for the workmen drilling holes to hang the tracks for the theatrical curtains.

I shook my head and came back to reality. Teamwork, I thought. Dancing is teamwork. There is the leader and there is the partner who follows. I got it, I thought. "Team Building Through Dance!" I could sell this concept to all corporations! I picked up the phone and quickly dialed the marketing director at the bank and explained the program to her. She was thrilled.

"I booked our first "Team Building Through Dance" program!" I shouted to Eduardo and Arty as I ran to the middle of the studio making sure I didn't slip on the dusty floor. "Eduardo, mark your calendar for January 14, 2005. You'll teach a dance routine, and I will demonstrate how the lead/follow rule of dance applies to everyday business life." Eduardo looked at me and said "OK, we will discuss this in detail as we near the date. Right now, I have to concentrate on where to hang the mirrors."

"Have the mirrors been delivered?" I asked excitedly, as I looked around the studio. Don't we need to paint the walls first?"

"No, the mirrors aren't in yet, but I expect them to come next week, and yes, we will paint the walls before they are hung. First, we need to get this dumpster out of here," he said as he pretended to kick it with his foot.

I nodded. Arty yelled out "good job," and continued talking to the men installing the air conditioning system.

Looking at my calendar, I noticed that Thanksgiving was the following week. Oh my God, I thought. Dec. 14th is only three and a half weeks away. I tried to visualize the finished studio, but still only saw the raw space.

- ♪ ♪ ♪ -

"Arty will we open by Dec. 14th? It's only a little more than three weeks away," I said later that night as I was putting the steaks in the broiler for dinner.

"Things are looking a bit better," he said as he sat on the couch. "The bathrooms are gutted and the construction for the new bathrooms should begin right after Thanksgiving. Once they are done we can get the painters in. I prefer to wait to paint until after the...."

I tuned him out. I didn't want to hear once they get done with this or that, or prefer to wait until...Wait for what! We had to open December 14th. We just *had* to!

During dinner I continued to nag Arty as I handed him a plate for salad. "You must push the workmen harder. You must make it happen. My anxiety is driving me crazy."

"Stop it, stop nagging me!" he said and smacked his hand on the table. "I'm doing the best I can. Don't you think I want it finished as quickly as you do? The sooner it is finished, the sooner we can give lessons. And more important, the sooner we can start to make some money." His anger made me cower.

"OK, OK, don't yell," I said. I took a small bite of steak. "I can't help it. I promised we would be open for her party. What if we're not? What if I have to tell her to go somewhere else at the last minute?"

"I don't want to hear the what ifs! We'll figure it out somehow, but stop hounding me," Arty said as he poured himself another glass of wine. We remained silent while we finished dinner.

"I'm sorry Arty," I said. I joined him on the couch. "I'll try to keep my anxiety under control."

He put his arm around me and told me not to worry. I felt better for the moment and rested my head on his shoulder.

Thanksgiving came and went. Arriving at the studio the following Monday, I noticed a big change. The studio was clean, the dumpster was gone. The phone started to ring with people requesting appointments. Our guerilla marketing efforts worked and people from our "Let's Dance" program in the park had started to schedule their complimentary lessons. I gave Eduardo the schedule. Surprisingly, I felt somewhat relieved, but I was still worried. Stop it, stop worrying, I repeated to myself.

"Ro," Eduardo's voice interrupted my thoughts. "Look at this new program my friend developed in Miami," he said as he handed me a DVD. "It's called Cardio Salsa. It's a great way to keep your heart healthy while learning to dance."

Reading the description of the program, I said, "Wow! This is perfect. Learn Salsa, Merengue, and Cha Cha while increasing your heart rate. Put the music on, I want to sample it." I began to dance around as he played the 45-minute DVD.

After testing the Cardio Salsa DVD, I had to wipe the sweat off my brow. I put two fingers on my pulse to test my heart rate. "Eduardo, my heart rate is up, just where it should be. This is an amazing workout. I love it." Catching my breath, I said, "and it beats the boredom of the treadmill!" I hugged Eduardo.

Energized with new ideas, I thought, people could give up their gym membership and exercise at Soho Dance. If I promote dance as a healthy outlet, we could capture a huge market: all wellness institutions and fitness fanatics. I closed my eyes and visualized students smiling as they pumped their arms, their biceps bulged as if they were pumping iron as their feet moved in sync to the Latin rhythms. I jumped up with enthusiasm. "Let's Dance Wellness" was my latest creation.

I was proud as I looked at my accomplishments. I posted my list on the bulletin board and then glanced at the calendar. Oh my

God, I thought, it was the first week in December, and we only had two more weeks left before our opening! I hadn't been giving much attention to the progress in the studio and I wouldn't dare discuss it with Arty anymore—it was a boundary I had learned not to cross.

I stood up to look for Arty. He was at the far end of the studio talking to the electrician. I was pleasantly surprised as I walked back; the painters were almost done, the mirrors were being hung. I tapped Arty on his shoulder and said, "We're sure to be ready by the 14th, right?"

"Looking good, but no promises," he said. "The drapes will be hung at the beginning of next week and the artist will outline the graffiti on the wall in the main ballroom tomorrow." He turned away and went back to his conversation with the electrician.

What was left? I looked around. The painters were applying the final coat to both bathrooms. I hoped the fixtures would be installed soon. "When are the toilets and the sinks coming? Are they still on back-order?" I called out to Arty. He raised his hand as if to tell me to wait a minute,

"December 10th."

"What about the reception desk? The computers?" I rambled.

"*Not now*," Arty shouted. "Later."

- ♪ ♪ ♪ -

It was December 13th. The floors were glistening with new polyurethane, the theatrical drapes were hung, the artist was putting finishing touches on our graffiti wall, the marble top of the reception desk was held down with big wooden clamps to be sure it was secure, the bathrooms were finished, computers were set up with the software installed to book students, and wires hung from the ceiling waiting for the final installation of the lights by the electrician. I breathed a big sigh of relief.

I walked throughout the 5500 square foot space running my fingers gently across the mirrors, feeling the thickness of the drapes making sure they were tied back properly, opening the bathroom doors, and I laughed as I checked the small kitchen. Why did I need a kitchen anyway, I thought, I'm not going to cook! Everything was perfect and Soho Dance would have a soft opening on December 14th. The ever-present tightness in my shoulder blades finally disappeared.

Then as I made my way to the front of the studio I experienced a very strange phenomenon. It was as if I were having an out of body experience. My mother who had been gone more than twenty years came to me as if in a vision. I can't explain it, but her presence was real. Chills went through my spine, and I felt goose bumps rise on my arms. I looked to the heavens straining my eyes for a glimpse of her. "Rosann," I heard her call out softly. "I'm so proud of you." I rubbed my eyes to try and see her clearly. She was blurry, like a wispy cloud hovering over me. My eyes welled up with tears. Was this real, or was it my subconscious telling me that I wanted my mother with me? Although it was surreal, it allowed me to believe she was there and approved of my new venture. I took a deep breath, wiped away my tears of joy and walked to the front of the studio. I couldn't get the smile off my face.

It was 9:00 p.m. and music filled the studio. I remember sitting behind the reception desk that still had the big wooden clamps on it. I remember tilting my head so I could see the electrician hook up the last set of track lights. Sitting next to one of the instructors, I looked at her and smiled as we watched the electrician come down the ladder and turn on the switch. "I'm finished," he said, adjusting his tool belt.

Arty walked out of the kitchen holding a bottle of champagne in one hand and champagne flutes in the other. "Let's celebrate," he said as he made his way up front.

All the instructors and the electrician gathered around the desk. Pop went the cork and Arty poured the champagne. "To Soho Dance, the hottest dance studio in New York City. Long live those dancin' feet!" We raised our glasses and said, "Cheers!"

On December 14, 2004, Soho Dance officially opened its doors. The reception area was filled with flowers: a vase of red roses sat on the of the desk, two poinsettia plants rested on the center windowsill, and our red upholstered seating cubes that resembled square ottomans faced the ballroom. Three flat screen TVs were hung to the left of the reception desk where two of them played videos of dance routines. The middle screen said "Welcome to Soho Dance."

Members of the networking group started arriving between 7:30 and 8:00 p.m. I was overwhelmed with excitement. "Welcome to Soho Dance where you will take A Step Out of the Ordinary," I said as I shook their hands. "The coat room is to your left and there is a table set up with refreshments in the main part of the studio," I said as I pointed to the ballroom.

My body tingled with goose bumps as I watched the attendees mingle. I must be dreaming, I thought. Is Soho Dance really open?

Eduardo interrupted my thoughts. "Let's get started," he said, looking at his watch.

"May I hold a brief meeting before your program starts?" Liz asked as we walked toward the reception area.

"Of course," I told her.

After conducting business, Liz thanked us for hosting their holiday party and introduced me. "Did you bring your dancin' feet?" I asked. Everyone laughed. "It's show time." I pointed to Eduardo.

Each instructor performed a routine. Some did the Cha Cha, some danced Salsa, and two other couples did the Hustle. The applause echoed throughout the studio as the instructors all took a bow.

"And now it's your turn," Eduardo said. The instructors brought members of the group on to the dance floor. Some shied away, but ultimately everyone stood up.

"One," Eduardo said as he demonstrated the basic steps of Salsa. "Good, let's try that again. One," he repeated. My mind drifted as he led them through a routine. I held Arty's hand as we watched the group dance. Was this real? Is this really my dance studio? I looked at Arty and kissed him on the cheek. "We did it, we did it," I whispered.

- ♪ ♪ ♪ -

It was the first week of January 2005 and hoards of people filtered in during prime time hours to take their group lessons. They were all smiles as they checked in. The phone continuously rang and we sold packages for both private and group classes. I thought I was being cute as I welcomed students and told them that they were starting the New Year on the 'right foot.'

Our four studios were filled with students learning different dance genres: Salsa in studio one, Cha Cha in studio two, the Hustle in studio three, and the Argentine Tango in studio four. Every hour, the level and type of dance changed, with the last class ending no later than 10:00 p.m. This sequence continued all week and we changed it around on a monthly basis. Eduardo was in charge of the monthly calendar and, depending on the response to each class, he made changes accordingly.

Arty, Eduardo, and I set the date of January 22, 2005 to hold the grand opening gala of Soho Dance. Knowing the studio could hold no more than 300 people, each of us limited our guest list to 100. The professionally designed invitation was "tres chic," and I smiled as I read it aloud;

You are cordially invited
to the Grand Opening Gala of Soho Dance
Saturday, January 22, 2005
8:00 p.m. 'til...
Join us for an evening of dining, dancing,
and entertainment
Festive Attire

"I'm glad we used red and black for the invitation. It's striking," I said to Arty turning the paper over in my hands.

The responses came pouring in. "Arty, Eduardo, look at these responses," I said as I held up a stack of rsvp cards. "So far, 100 people have said yes." I went back to checking off my list.

Planning for the gala was exciting. I ordered tables and chairs, hired a caterer, and chose the decorations. We decided against a DJ, and instead, Eduardo hired a well-known twelve piece Latin band. Together, Eduardo and Arty planned the format and entertainment for the evening. The dance routines were choreographed and we decided that each teacher would perform his or her specialty. There would be ten performances in all.

The excitement built as we neared the 22nd. The teachers practiced their routines daily and we had a dress rehearsal two days before the gala. The tables, chairs, and tablecloths were delivered. I went over the food list with the caterer and at the last minute, I decided to hire a photographer. Arty also wanted this night to be extra special and ordered outdoor beams of light that would light up the sky and bring attention to our opening from miles away. It would be like a Hollywood opening. Everything was in order, or so I thought.

The day before the gala we decorated the studio and turned the ballroom into a lounge. The round cocktail tables were covered with long black tablecloths and we had black and red balloons as our centerpieces. Candles and small vases filled with red roses were placed on the makeshift bar, and the two adjacent serving tables. As we left that evening, I looked around. "The place looks great," I said to Arty as we waited for the elevator. "Maybe I'll go into event planning." I laughed to myself.

The phone rang the minute we got home. It was Eduardo. "Did you hear the weather report? They're predicting snow tomorrow, they're predicting a blizzard," he said in a halting voice.

"What," I screamed. "Arty did you hear the weather report; Eduardo said there's going to be a snow storm."

"What are we going to do?" Eduardo asked. "We have 300 people coming to our gala, we can't cancel the food, it's too late and what about the band?"

I handed the phone to Arty. "Calm down," Arty said. "I'm sure the "snowstorm" will only be a few flakes and then turn to rain. You know the weather men are almost never right." Arty sat down. "Get a good night's sleep and we'll meet you at the studio in the morning."

"Who had time to listen to the weather reports?" I said as I walked to the closet and hung up my coat. The possibility of a snow storm had never entered my mind.

I started my what ifs. "What if there is a big snowstorm? Will anyone come to our opening? What about the outdoor spotlights? What about the food and booze? What about the band?"

"Enough," Arty burst out. "We'll worry about it tomorrow. We can't control it, what will be, will be."

Arty sounded like my mother. Thinking of her made me feel calmer.

The sky was overcast when we arrived at the studio in the morning. "It's going to snow," I said to Arty as we entered the studio. "I know it. I feel it. What are we going to do?"

"We are having the gala," he told me with determination. "Whoever comes, will come." And as he stepped off the elevator he began to sing, "Let It Snow." He pretended to feel the snowflakes and opened his palms toward the ceiling.

"Arty, please stop joking with me. What are we going to do?"

"I'm not joking and stop taking this so seriously, it's only snow; it's not life or death. I promise it will be a great party." He walked behind the desk to check the phone messages.

The phone didn't stop ringing with people asking if the party was still on. "Yes, yes, yes," I repeated again and again. "Be sure to bring your dancin' shoes."

It was noon when the snow began to fall. By the afternoon, there were three to four inches on the ground and the meteorologists were reporting blizzard conditions. I blocked the negativity out of my mind. At least public transportation is still running, I thought.

The caterer arrived at 5:00 p.m. The chef began to prep the food and his staff set up the bar. Friends and family sent congratulatory flowers and balloons. The studio looked more festive than ever. Everything was falling into place and I started to relax.

I took one last look at the studio before I dressed. I had bought a fabulous red strapless chiffon dress with a handkerchief hemline sure to swirl with every turn. I had my hair and makeup done professionally earlier in the day and at 7:00 p.m. I slipped my dress over my head and let it slide down my hips. I touched up my hair and smiled as I looked in the mirror. I feel like a movie star, I thought. I should be on a red carpet. I laughed as I stepped out from the bathroom. Arty's eyes opened wide and his mouth fell open when he saw me. I remember his expression when he saw me in my wedding dress for the first time, this time his expression was the same. He looked so handsome in his black suit and red shirt. We are an elegant couple, I thought.

The outdoor spotlight made the snowflakes appear larger than they were. The intense blue and white beams rotating on the base of a pick up truck lit up the sky. Crowds of people started arriving at 8:00 p.m. and stamped their snow-covered boots onto a mat.

They took off their boots, checked them with their coats at the coat check, and put on shoes. The music from the band drew them onto the dance floor.

As I looked around, I couldn't believe the size of the crowd. 250 people had braved the cold and snow and had joined us to celebrate our grand opening.

"May I have this dance?" Arty asked as he took me in his arms. I felt as if I were living in a fantasy as Arty led me across the floor. I was filled with contentment and joy.

The show started at 9:00 p.m. Eduardo welcomed everyone and, after making a few remarks, introduced the first couple of instructors who opened the program with the Hustle. Then came in quick succession the West Coast Swing, Argentine Tango, Cha Cha, Rumba, Fox Trot, and finally, the Quickstep. The costumes all sparkled as the lights hit the glitter on the dresses. Just as I finished applauding the last dancers, I heard Eduardo say, "And now ladies and gentlemen, I bring you the stars of the show, Rosann and Arthur Levy who will perform the Salsa."

I was in total shock, but Arty gave me no time to react. He took me in his arms and we performed. At the end of our routine Arty put me into a dip. "Don't drop me," I whispered. The applause was deafening as we bowed. My body shook with excitement.

The crowd shouted, "Encore, encore." We both smiled and took another bow. The show closed with Eduardo and his partner dancing Salsa. It was an amazing performance, especially when Eduardo flipped his partner into the air.

The grand opening of Soho Dance was grander than I ever could have imagined. The blizzard of 2005 only added to the magic of the evening.

- ♪ ♪ ♪ -

The grand opening set the tone for Soho Dance. I planned special themed events around holidays: "Dance and Romance" on Valentines Day, "Put a little Irish in Your Jig," "Bunny Hop into Spring," "Swing into Summer" and my favorite, "Salsa With Santa." I enjoyed being an event planner.

The students became my friends, and over the months, I began to think of them as my extended family. There was an unspoken trust and understanding that bonded our relationships, with dance as the common thread that we shared.

I remember Diane, a woman in her early sixties who came every day for lessons. Although she was a short stocky woman, she was very light on her feet. I was amazed as I watched her dance; she moved remarkably well. I remember watching her learn the Jitterbug. She hopped and bounced around the dance floor and used the motion of her pelvis to swing her hips. When the teacher picked her up and shifted her from side to side and then slid her between his legs, my mouth hung open. Secretly I wished I could do that. Diane loved Soho Dance and told me it was her home away from home. I thought of her as Soho Dance's mascot.

- ♪ ♪ ♪ -

Janet wanted to learn the waltz. "I am celebrating my 65th birthday next month and I want to learn the Waltz and the Fox Trot.

My husband is taking me to the Rainbow Room," she said as she purchased her package of ten private lessons. "I'm looking forward to dancing to the sounds of the big band and twirling around on their famous revolving dance floor."

"That's exciting," I said. "Would you like to perform at our guest night on your birthday? We hold them every week and invite students to perform the routines they have learned."

"I'd love it," she responded. "Can I invite my family?"

"Absolutely." I took out our calendar and put her name on the list.

Janet's performance was amazing. She looked stunning in her black chiffon gown as she glided along the dance floor. She arched her back and maintained a perfect frame for the Waltz. When she finished her performance, her husband handed her a bouquet of red roses. He kissed her and said, "You're the best sixty-five-year-old dancer I know."

- ♪ ♪ ♪ -

Henry was promoting gym memberships and had a table on the street with brochures advertising the new club that had opened down the block from our studio. On my way back from lunch, I stopped to talk with him. He was a tall, good looking guy. His tight tee shirt clung to his six-pack abs. He was the picture of fitness. Introducing myself we spoke about cross-marketing the fitness center and Soho Dance. He said he would speak with his boss and we made an appointment to meet at Soho Dance later that week. He had no idea what was in store for him.

"No, no," Henry said as he stood at our reception desk. "I have two left feet. I'm dyslexic. I could never learn to dance."

"I guarantee you will. Take a complimentary half hour lesson and if you don't learn the basic steps, I'll stop nagging you," I said as I introduced him to a cute perky instructor. He took one look at her and said, "OK, I'll give it a try."

Henry went on to be one of the very best students in the studio. He spent every free moment he had taking lessons. He performed on numerous guest nights and became one of our biggest promoters.

- ♪ ♪ ♪ -

Monica was a young girl in her early twenties. She came to the studio one afternoon and sat in the reception area for an hour watching the other students take their lessons. After observing her for a while I introduced myself. "Hi, I'm Rosann, one of the owners," I said as I took the seat next to her.

She sat silently for a few more minutes. "I would love to dance, but I am deathly afraid that I'll look like a fool," she said. She turned her head and went back to watching the lesson.

I took her hand in mine. She was shaking. "Dancing is fun," I said. "I promise you the moment you step out on the dance floor, your shaking will stop and you will be smiling." Eduardo walked into the reception area and I introduced him to Monica. "Eduardo will take good care of you, trust me. If you don't enjoy yourself you never have to step out on the dance floor ever again."

"May I have the pleasure of this dance?" Eduardo asked as he escorted Monica on to the dance floor. Her half hour lesson changed her life. Not only did she book a twenty lesson package, but she also brought her mother back later that week.

I knew I had changed Monica's life forever and knew that her mother was happy watching her daughter enjoy herself.

- ♪ ♪ ♪ -

In the spring of our first year, we learned about one of the biggest dance competitions in the country called the Miami Salsa Congress. It was a competition for dancers in all genres at all levels, and Diane, Monica, Harry, Janet, and twenty other students signed up to participate in the competition. They bought special dance lesson packages that focused on the technical aspects of the dances as well as on perfecting the choreographed routines. Each of the students were placed in categories: beginner, intermediate, and advanced and beginner, intermediate and advanced over forty.

Watching the students learn the steps and rehearse the techniques made me think of them as professionals. But competitions were difficult as they revved up emotions. The students were perfectionists and if they did a step incorrectly or missed a beat they'd react. Some would stomp out of the studio, others would cry.

I remember Marilyn. She was a tall blonde who wore short skirts that accentuated her long legs. She signed on to compete but was very hard on herself. She came every day after work to rehearse and treated her sessions as though she were training for the Olympics. I loved watching her dance as she was smooth and graceful, but she didn't see herself that way. When she made a mistake she'd cry hysterically. I'd try to soothe her. "It's only a dance," I said as I handed her some tissues. "This is about having fun."

She nodded her head and tried to smile through her tears.

But Marilyn wasn't alone. A number of the other female students broke down as well. I began to think this was a girl thing.

"Uh oh. Here come the water works," Eduardo told Arty. He wanted no part of the crying and walked to the back office while I tried to calm the girls.

Despite the anguish of preparing for competition, Miami was an amazing experience. It surprised me that although we were the new kid on the block, we had more students competing and a larger cheering section than any other dance studio there. I blocked out two large round tables in the ballroom close to the dance floor to be sure our dancers could see and hear us as we cheered them on.

"Go Soho," we shouted each time our students' names were called. Diane, Harry, Janet, Monica, Marilyn each won two or more medals and fifteen others came home with at least one. I reserved a hospitality suite in the hotel to celebrate and congratulated all for a job well done. Soho Dance certainly left its mark on Miami!

- ♪ ♪ ♪ -

Every day, there were new opportunities for our students and for us: there were competitions all around the country, there were lessons at local dance clubs, performances at guest night, Funky Friday hustle nights, the list was endless.

But the highlight of my first year at Soho Dance was when we were asked to participate in the American Cancer Society's Relay for Life at Shea Stadium in May of 2005. The Relay for Life honors cancer survivors, pays tribute to the lives lost, and supports those who are faced with the dreadful disease.

I was approached by one of our students who asked if we would give complimentary Salsa lessons to the participants during the afternoon. Without hesitation, I said yes. "In addition to giving complimentary lessons, I will form the Soho Dance Team and all the money I raise will be given to the cancer society." I said. "And I'll do even better than that. I will print up promo cards and offer a half hour lesson for the cost of $20, and all the monies raised will be donated, too," I told her. "The cancer society is my charity of choice. I have a son who is a cancer survivor and I will do anything to help stamp out this disease."

"Thank you so much," she said. "The Soho Dance Team can walk around the warning track at Shea at the same time as all the teams. All you need is a banner and the name of a song you want to hear as you walk the track. Also all the survivors are walking too, so ask your son if he would like to participate."

I gave her a big hug and told her I would be in touch as we neared the date. She left me with all the particulars and I immediately formed the Soho Dance Team.

- ♪ ♪ ♪ -

It was a beautiful day with the sun shining brightly. This was God's way of telling me everything was all right, I thought. Standing in the bleachers at Shea Stadium with twenty-five of my students who had signed up for the Soho Dance Team, I cried as I watched my son, Gary, walk among other cancer survivors, holding the hands of his two sons, Andrew, five, and Michael, two, as they walked around the warning track at Shea. I smiled through my tears as I watched Mr. Met, the Mets team mascot follow and throw a ball to the kids. I held Arty's hand tightly.

"I am so happy," I said as I looked around at my team. "Thank you for supporting me and my family." We reached for each other and hugged.

When it was our team's turn to walk, a group of us held the Soho banner high. "Look, look there's our team lit up on the scoreboard," I said as we danced around the warning track to the Bee Gees song, "Stayin' Alive." It was truly a day to celebrate.

- ♪ ♪ ♪ -

The spring, summer and fall went by quickly and before I realized it the holiday season was upon us. Our "Salsa with Santa" was a big hit. All the instructors wore Santa caps and one of them taught the lesson dressed as Santa. His belly shook madly every time he did a turn.

"I can't believe at the end of this month we will have been opened for one year already. It went by so fast," I said to Eduardo and Arty. "Let's have an anniversary party. It doesn't have to be as grand as our opening gala, but I think it's important to acknowledge our success." They both agreed.

The date was set for Saturday, January 21, 2006. This time I listened to the weather forecast every day the week before the party.

Arty, Eduardo, and I met right after the New Year to plan the party. Instead of a formal invitation, I designed a festive flyer and posted the event on our website. We decided on finger food and wines rather than a full dinner with an open bar.

"Ro, Arty, I want to choreograph a special performance for you. You deserve it and I want to show off your talent," Eduardo said as he swiveled his chair to face us. "I'll work with you. Just tell me what dance you want to perform."

I liked the idea. "Arty what do you think? What dance would you want to do?" I asked.

"I'm not sure I want to perform. I like giving the students the opportunity. It makes them feel important and besides it keeps them buying lessons." Arty paused, "Remember, it's always about the money."

I ignored his remark and said, "Come on Arty. We don't get a chance to dance that much any more and at our gala our performance was impromptu. It will be fun performing a choreographed routine, just like professionals." I stood up. "Please, please," I begged.

Eduardo chimed in, "There will only be five performances, and aside from you and Rosann, the rest will be performed by our top students. I promise I will choreograph something amazing; a dance routine you will never forget. What dance do you want to perform? Do you want to Rumba, Hustle, Cha Cha, Salsa..."

Arty interrupted. "OK, OK. I love the Fox Trot, but I love Salsa too."

Before Arty said another word, Eduardo jumped up. "That's

it. I'll choreograph a Fox Trot that opens into a Salsa. What a great idea." He sat down, put on his headset and began to listen to music.

"How exciting," I said. "But I don't understand how it will work."

"No worries, leave it up to me." He went back to his music.

The next day, we started rehearsal. Eduardo took us to the ballroom and turned on the CD. We listened as Frank Sinatra sang "It Happened in Monterey."

"This will be your opening" Eduardo said and directed us. "Stand apart. Arty, reach your left arm out and grab Rosann's right hand; when the music begins pull her in close to you and take her in your arms. Do you get it?"

We stood under the Soho Dance sign. Arty reached out for me and when the music started he spun me and pulled me in close to him. "That's good," Eduardo said. "Now I am going to take you into a promenade but do not, I repeat, do not begin your promenade walk until you hear Frank Sinatra begin singing 'It Happened in Monterey,' otherwise you'll be off beat. Arty watch while I dance with Rosann." Eduardo pulled me in and led me into the promenade when Frank began to sing.

"I got it. Start the music again and let me give it a try," Arty said as he reached for my hand.

Every day, we did a little bit more and by the end of two weeks, Eduardo had taught us how to break into Salsa. "Wow, this is amazing," I said as I faced Arty and held his hands. I began to laugh as we did our Salsa moves; the cross body lead, the copa, and ended with a dip.

We rehearsed for two hours every day trying to perfect our routine. One week before the party, we were ready. "Arty, we're like Fred Astaire and Ginger Rogers. All you need is a top hat and cane," I said laughing. "I must buy a new dress, and then I'll really be like Ginger Rogers." I went to get my coat. "See you later."

The day arrived and we were ready. I picked out a pink shirt for Arty to wear with his black suit, and he put a matching hankie in his jacket pocket. I bought a sleeveless black silk dress with beads dotting the hemline with a low cut v-neck in the front and back. As I did for the gala, I had my hair and makeup professionally done at the beauty salon. As I looked in my bedroom mirror, I thought, I should be on the cover of *Glamour* Magazine.

"Wow, you look great," Arty said as he helped me on with my coat. "Let's go Ginger."

We got to the studio at 7:00 p.m. Our guests had already started to arrive. The students who were performing were busy getting dressed and fixing their hair and makeup. The food was placed on tables in the front and the back of the studio with bottles of red and white wine ready to be poured. A pang of nervousness sent chills through my body when I saw the chairs set up in the ballroom. We hadn't set up any chairs at our grand opening gala; people stood or sat around the stage. Why did we have chairs now? Was it because we were performing a choreographed routine like professionals? The word choreographed scared me. We weren't professionals. Was the audience expecting to see professionals dance? Oh my God, what if I mess up or step on Arty's feet? My anxiety continued to build.

I paced back and forth making sure that everything was in

place. "Rosann, you look stunning," Diane said. "Let me get a photo of you and Arty."

"I'll be up front in a minute and you can take all the pictures you want," I told her. I went into the bathroom and checked my hair and makeup. I put on some fresh lip gloss and pressed my lips together. I'm ready for photos now, I thought.

I grabbed Arty who was talking to Eduardo. "Arty, Diane wants to take some pictures of us, please come up front with me," I said as I pulled at his jacket sleeve. "Are you nervous?" I asked as we walked to the reception area.

"No, what's there to be nervous about? It'll be fun. Stop worrying,' he said.

Diane and a number of other students snapped pictures. As the cameras flashed, I thought, it's the paparazzi—we must be famous.

"It's show-time," Eduardo said, and summoned everyone to take their seats. The crowd refilled their glasses with wine and entered the ballroom.

"Thank you all for coming and helping us to celebrate the first anniversary of Soho Dance. We have an exciting show planned and you will have plenty of time to dance after the performances. But before we begin we have someone we want to honor for her loyalty and support; Diane, please step up to the stage," Eduardo said as he pointed to Diane who was sitting in the front row.

Diane was so taken by surprise that she began to hyperventilate, so much so, that we were briefly scared that she was going to pass out. But Arty and Eduardo helped her out of her seat and up to the stage. "Catch your breath," Arty said as he held her so she wouldn't fall.

After a few moments she caught her breath. Eduardo, Arty and I presented her with a dozen roses and a framed Certificate of Appreciation and thanked her again for her support.

"I'm so flattered; nobody has ever done this for me before. I'm speechless." The audience applauded and she began to smile. "Thank you, thank you all from the bottom of my heart. Soho Dance will always be a part of my life and I will treasure this moment forever." She waved as Arty helped her off the stage.

"And now I want to present you with what you've been waiting for," Eduardo began. "You all know Rosann and Arty, and I'm sure you are aware of their passion for dance. They are the heart and soul of Soho Dance. They have been like family to me as I know they are for many of you." Eduardo held back tears. "It is with great pleasure that I introduce the true stars of Soho Dance—Rosann and Arthur Levy.

Arty walked in from the right and I walked in from the left as everyone applauded and we took our place on the stage. It was a dreamlike moment and I wasn't sure I was really there. Arty reached for my hand, the music started, and he pulled me in close to him. My heart began to palpitate and the rapid beat vibrated in my chest like a kettle-drum. The tingling sensation in my fingertips was moving to my forearms and my toes felt numb.

Wait for Frank to sing, wait for Frank to sing, I repeated to myself. Arty and I paused and suddenly, we heard Frank's voice belt out, "It Happened in Monterey." It was our cue and I felt the pressure of Arty's hand on my left shoulder blade as he led me into our promenade. I gripped his hand tightly.

Momentarily, I felt Arty and I were there alone dancing to the melodic voice of Frank Sinatra. With the spotlight hitting my face, I noticed my dress shimmer and felt the silk lining move subtly around my hips as we glided along the stage. Glancing at the audience, I saw lots of smiling faces and then caught a glimpse of my daughter out of the corner of my eye. Her beautiful smile encouraged me and she waved. As we danced, I felt like a balloon filled with helium floating high up into the sky.

Holding me closer, Arty took me into a right turn and led me with a continuous flowing movement. With each step, I relinquished control. I had an adrenaline rush and felt exhilarated as the endorphins in my body give me a powerful uplift as if Arty and I were in a tandem free fall.

Arty took me back into the promenade and we danced diagonally toward the center of the stage. As we heard Frank's voice fade out Arty spun me to his left. We paused and stood in front of the audience with our arms outstretched as if we were about to take a bow.

In a split second, the music changed from the romantic sounds of the crooner to the Latin rhythm of the Buena Vista Social Club and with that Arty and I faced one another, grabbed hands, and immediately began to dance our Salsa routine. The audience was caught by surprise.

Just as they thought something was about to end, something new had begun.

I heard the roar of their voices and the applause almost deafened my ears. Our routine ended with a dip, only this time I didn't whisper "don't drop me." There was a standing ovation as we took our bows. Arty and I were glowing and I felt that the smiles on our faces would stay with us forever. The enchanting evening was magical.

In that moment I had an epiphany that my life was much like the Hustle, a fusion of many different steps, styles, and emotions, touched by the rhythms of Latin dance. Just as the Hustle is a partner dance, I knew that my evolving "dance" through life, would not mean much to me without the constant, reassuring, and loving presence of Arty by my side.

- ♪ ♪ ♪ -

I can't explain why I like to take on new challenges, like building a business, traveling to a foreign country, and learning all about its culture, or learning how to do the Hustle. Perhaps it's because the thought of something new is exciting and gets my juices flowing. Soho Dance was one of the biggest undertakings I have ever experienced, but a voice inside of me told me it was the right thing to do. I've learned to trust that voice.

The word retirement is not in my vocabulary. I am proud of my accomplishments and especially proud that I did something in my golden years to help people enjoy life to the fullest.

It is my hope that those who read my story know that just as *It's Never Too Late to Dance,* it's never too late to make choices for a better life.

I think about the Buena Vista Social Club and Omara Portunondo who continue to entertain; give back and bring happiness to people around the world. I believe that they inspired me.

Rosann Levy

I am grateful to have had the chance to touch so many lives and bring happiness to people of all ages, all ethnicities and skills through the world of dance.

My Dance Continues...

I cried as I finished the last chapter of my story. As I shut down the computer I began to sob. I couldn't understand why, as I truly enjoyed the experience of writing about my life—it purified me emotionally and spiritually. In continuing my life's dance, Arty took me to a neighboring restaurant to celebrate. My emotional state awry, my laughter turned into tears and back to laughter as I sipped my wine, yet I was proud to add this to my long list of accomplishments.

Arty and I owned Soho Dance for two and one half years. We decided to sell after we moved to Norwalk, Connecticut to spend more time with our children and grandchildren. Just before we sold the studio we enjoyed one last dance on national TV—*The Morning Show with Mike and Juliet*; Fox Five New York. Much to our surprise, Len and Bruno, the judges from *Dancing with the Stars*; a show we had never seen, critiqued our routine. Though I miss the gratification of watching the students master dance steps and routines, Arty and I enjoy dancing at socials, parties, clubs, when we travel, and now look forward to watching *Dancing With The Stars* every week.

Rosann Levy

I believe everything happens for a reason; our move to Connecticut enables us to see our grandchildren regularly; we bought a boat, named it the Ro-Sea, and enjoy boating on the Long Island Sound exploring little towns and villages both on Long Island and Connecticut. Arty got his license as a residential real estate appraiser, and I work part time as the merchandise manager in the boutique at my daughter's yoga studio; Saraswatis Yoga Joint. But as true entrepreneurs, we decided to embark on yet another dance and opened The Roart Group, LLC, a small and family business consulting firm in which we continue to help people achieve their goals and lead a more fulfilling life. So, the dance never ends, but continues to teach us new steps that make our lives more meaningful. I don't know where my life will take me next; perhaps another book, or some other new challenge, what I do know is *It's Never Too Late To Dance*, and I will keep on dancing.

About the Author

Rosann Levy, along with her husband, Arthur, founded Soho Dance in 2004, one of the hottest Latin ballroom dance studios in Manhattan. Prior to opening her Latin ballroom dance studio, Rosann worked with her husband and two sons in their boutique accounting firm. As Director of Marketing, she was instrumental in enabling the firm to sell to one of the top 25 accounting firms in the country in just 12 years, so that she and her husband could retire from the family business. She also was President of the National Association of Women Business Owners and founded and was President of the Family Business Council of Greater New York, a non-profit organization that addressed issues facing family run businesses. She wrote a seminal article, "Growing the Firm—and Growing the Marriage," which was published in *Family Business Magazine*, and the publisher's Family Business Handbook, *Building Strong Family Business Teams*. She has been honored numerous times by the New York Chamber of Commerce & Industry, the New York Society of Association Executives and the American Marketing Association.

She has appeared on *The Morning Show With Mike & Juliet*

(Fox 5) and *Good Day New York* and was interviewed by Joan Hamburg and her daughter on WOR radio. She was featured in *Ebony* magazine and has been cited in various business publications including *The New York Times* and *Crain's New York Business*. She has also had guest appearances on the *Today* show, CNN, CNBC, *Live at 5* (NBC), and other television programs.

She continues to be outspoken in the business community spreading information on how to achieve self-transformation and change in her "golden years." Rosann has been married forty-nine years, is the mother of four children, the grandmother of nine, and resides with her husband in Norwalk, Connecticut.

It's Never Too Late To Dance ...

For more information regarding Rosann Levy and her work,
visit her web site: **www.itsnevertoolatetodance.com**.

Additional copies of this book may be purchased online from
LegworkTeam.com; Amazon.com; BarnesandNoble.com;
Borders.com, or via the author's web site,
www.itsnevertoolatetodance.com.

You can also obtain a copy of the book by visiting L.I. Books or
ordering it from your favorite bookstore.